T5-AWK-763

The POLITICAL ECONOMY of DISTRIBUTION

The POLITICAL ECONOMY of DISTRIBUTION

Equality versus Inequality

MICHAEL DON WARD

Elsevier · New York

NEW YORK · OXFORD

Exclusive Distribution
throughout the World by
Greenwood Press, Westport,
Ct. U.S.A.

Elsevier North Holland, Inc.
52 Vanderbilt Avenue, New York, New York 10017

Distributors outside the United States and Canada:

Thomond Books
(A Division of Elsevier/North-Holland Scientific Publishers, Ltd.)
P.O. Box 85
Limerick, Ireland

© 1978 by Elsevier North-Holland, Inc.

Library of Congress Cataloging in Publication Data

Ward, Michael D., 1948–
    The political economy of distribution: equality versus inequality

    Based on the author's thesis, Northwestern University.
    Bibliography: p.
    Includes index.
    1. Income distribution. 2. Equality. I. Title.
    HC79.I5W38   339.2   78-15755
    ISBN 0-444-99054-2

Manufactured in the United States of America

Designed by Loretta Li

DISCARDED

WIDENER UNIVERSITY

WIDENER UNIVERSITY
WOLFGRAM
LIBRARY
CHE----

to S.L.W.

Contents

List of Figures

List of Tables

Acknowledgments

It seems only fitting to note that this book on inequality was marked by the unselfish contributions of many people. These contributions to the "net" product were substantial. I have been aided by skilled and intelligent researchers whose work in this area provided the foundation for my work, critical and insightful tutors, and understanding, encouraging friends and companions.

Tong Whan Park has been a great friend and adviser throughout this project, begun as my doctoral thesis. In this study and others, his ability to provide a clear, succinct, and too often telling critique rarely failed him. Kenneth Janda provided particularly insightful comments on an early version of the manuscript, as did James Caporaso. Ted Gurr's standards of excellence are well known; I have benefited immensely from his work, as well as from his comments about my work. Farid Abolfathi deserves special thanks; not only did he provide considerable encouragement and friendship, he also made available a substantial amount of data that was collected for his own doctoral project. Northwestern University provided considerable assistance in the form of institutional support, including both fellowships and a lion's share of our department's computer budget. The preparation of the manuscript was supported by the Gordon Scott Fulcher Chair of Decision Making at Northwestern University.

Harold Guetzkow has been supportive, helpful, and provocative in ways too numerous to detail fully. I have been able to use his insight and comments to make this a much better piece of research. His moral and financial support in this enterprise is gratefully acknowledged and warmly appreciated. Norma Wood also deserves thanks for her meticulous and understanding help. Warren Silver also aided in the final preparation of the manuscript.

My association with Elsevier has been delightful in every way. William L. Gum and Ethel Langlois were supportive not only of the book itself but also of our decision to utilize state-of-the-art computer technology in converting my machine-readable manuscript into proofs.

Hayward Alker deserves special mention. Though he doubtless has many disagreements with positions I have taken in this work, his probing comments have been instrumental in suggesting revisions. More importantly, his ever insightful and provocative ideas have suggested new approaches to and analyses of the question of international inequality which will, I hope, come to fruition in the future.

Foreword

This book is about social and economic inequalities at the domestic
level and their causes. In attempting to develop an explanation of
domestic inequalities, Dr. Ward tries to mesh, rather than merely
juxtapose, domestic and international sources of inequalities. He also
draws freely on explanations centering on the political system (e.g.,
the impact of public policies upon inequality) and those relying more
on the private sector (e.g., the link between economic growth and
inequalities).

The Political Economy of Distribution is timely but hopefully not
time-bound. It fits with and contributes to a growing body of literature
on the relationship between economic growth, redistributive political
action, and internal inequalities. Though the evidence is presented in
a statistical idiom, the spirit of the book is neither hostile to nor aloof
from the case study literature. Indeed, the author both learns from
and contributes to that literature. What can be summarized and expressed in general terms by statistical techniques is so expressed;
what cannot be readily summarized is carefully probed on a more-
detailed plane.

The questions posed concerning the causes of inequality are interesting ones as they are questions to which we must attach the
utmost importance on normative grounds. The problems, however, as
noted by the author himself, are immense. There is inconsistent evidence concerning the relationship between level and rate of development and inequality. When one considers that a *rate* is merely a series
of levels viewed in relation to one another and that a *level* is merely a
snapshot of a single component of a rate, this discrepancy poses a

troubling starting point for the analysis of inequality. In addition, the data base—the ore with which one works—is of poor quality. This is due partly to missing data, partly to the existence of incorrect data. Finally, there is the problem that most of the findings that do exist are isolated from one another, presented in bivariate rather than multivariate form, and derived from studies which assume *ceteris paribus* rather than assure this by conducting research in a controlled way (e.g., by either controlling the setting or the analysis).

The author attacks these problems head on. To give the essence of his approach without providing a summary, I will stress two themes of this book: the emphasis on contributing to our body of knowledge in a cumulative rather than discontinuous way, and the attempt to treat the subject matter in a synthetic as well as analytic way.

Both of these themes merit a brief word. The author's concern with the cumulation of research findings leads him to a careful examination of the causes in inequality in light of existing evidence and literature. He takes great pains to start from what we know, to scrutinize his own findings against that backdrop, and to refine the arguments and testing procedures where this is possible. Thus, the starting point of the analysis is provided by the seminal contributions of Simon Kuznets, Irma Adelman and Hollis Chenery concerning the relationship between development, growth, and inequality.

Their insights and findings provide the "germ" around which the remainder of the book takes shape. From here the author carefully incorporates additional variables. We have a chapter on the importance of political and institutional factors (Chapter 4) and one on the importance of the international system in affecting domestic inequalities (Chapter 5). In carrying out this complicated task, the author successfully integrates explanations based on economic and political variables.

The author's concerns were both analytical and synthetic. There were times when puzzles or unresolved questions were due to inadequate distinctions in the existing literature, as for example in the curvilinear relationship between economic development and inequality. This question called for further analysis and for identification of variables that mediate the relationship between economic variables and inequality. The approach here was to "unpackage" this relation, to look carefully inside, and to suggest what might have been left out. This led naturally to a focus on political variables as well as to a focus on the political economy of the international system and the ways in which it impinges on domestic inequality. This analytic orientation is accompanied by the contrapuntal theme of synthesis. The author is concerned not only with analytic refinements but with providing a coherent, overall explanation of inequality. This leads him to reject a piecemeal approach to the data analysis and to adopt the contrary position of reporting the evidence in a multivariate and wholistic way, with due account taken of the large number of factors that must be considered even when examining simpler relationships.

This synthetic approach is best illustrated by the author's treatment of the international causes of inequality, particularly the way these arguments and findings are incorporated or "built into" the foregoing analysis rather than merely appended or "layered on." In examining the external causes of domestic inequality, he does not leave behind the work carried out in previous chapters. Instead, he continually challenges, amends, and refines his work in light of the arguments and evidence presented in the sections on the domestic sources in inequality.

Happily, this is not one of those books about which one is obliged to say: "It doesn't answer any questions but it certainly creates a large research agenda." Though confirmation of theories regarding such complicated questions must always be regarded as tentative, there are a number of notable findings in this work. The probing analysis of the curvilinear relationship between economic development and inequality is an important contribution that advances our knowledge of the mechanisms of development. In addition, the findings concerning the relative potency of external (international) variables and the way in which the external environment dampens the influence of domestic policy variables are both important and provocative. The thrust of the evidence strengthens the hand of those who have long been arguing the impossibility of viewing developmental and distributive policies solely in domestic terms.

James A. Caporaso

Andrew W. Mellon Professor
of International Studies
University of Denver

Research Strategy

1

1.1 INTRODUCTION

By most accounts the gap between the rich and the poor is growing. This seems true at both the international level, as between wealthy and impoverished nations, and the domestic level, as between wealthy and poor individuals and groups. More pessimistic accounts assess the growth to be very large. While it seems that few polities will actually experience large decreases in the aggregate level of material wealth during the next twenty to thirty years, from 1970 to the year 2000, it is apparent that the differential growth rates of the rich and the poor within countries may tend to increase the gap between them. This "fact" is perhaps the one aspect of global political economy on which both radical and conservative scholars can agree (Woodhouse, 1972).

There is apparently a similar agreement on the increasing interconnectedness of global actors. There is no single necessary consequence of this trend, although one plausible result is that there will be an attendant growth in the interaction felt across the various levels within the global system. International events and processes will have greater and increasingly subtle effects upon the events and processes which appear to some to be largely noninternational in scope, such as the purchase of gasoline. Thus, it seems likely that international influences will become more important in the affairs of individuals, and conversely, that domestic ones will become more critical in international affairs.

Most recently, there has been considerable interest in studies that attempt to mesh international and domestic explanations of political and economic phenomena. Some researchers were no doubt drawn to this position by the articles on linkage politics in the volume edited by James Rosenau (1969). More still have found inspiration in the works of dependency theorists such as Dos Santos (1970), who have sought an essentially international explanation of why Latin American economies have typically remained at such "low" levels of development throughout the twentieth century. Similarly, recent work on the role of transnational forms of organization, notably the multinational corporation, by Keohane and Nye (1972) among others, has illustrated the incompleteness of explaining domestic political phenomena without also studying organizations and groups which themselves tend to transcend the boundaries of the nation-state. On the other side of the same coin, the bureaucratic politics paradigm (Allison, 1971) argues that foreign policies are greatly influenced by organizational subunits of national governments. Another tack has been undertaken by those scholars who argue on theoretical grounds that there is sufficient diffusion of both ideas and institutions among polities, to make it impossible to understand patterns of political behavior from a perspective that does not include national and international patterns (Gillespie, 1970; Duvall, 1975).

All of these various thrusts into the problem of melding international and subnational politics, in one form or another, seek to cope with the inadequacies of behavioral and structural explanations that are not global in scope. As such they may be viewed as general system theoretic approaches which address not only the behaviors of elements within a system, but also the structure of that system itself and the constraints which it places upon its members.

This study is an attempt to begin the systematic examination of the interaction of international and domestic politics as they relate to one specific domain: the distribution of valued goods within the polity.

1.2 WHY STUDY THE DISTRIBUTION?

Quite simply, the motivation to study inequality is based upon four interrelated ideas. The first of these is sufficient to justify considerable inquiry on inequality, but taken as a whole they may be used to justify investigation within the specific context of both domestic (internal)

[2]

and international (external) explanations of political phenomena. High levels of inequality are strikingly visible within most groups of men, and accordingly, inequality is of considerable import for the bulk of classical modern poltical theory. Rawls' (1971) recent book and the phenomenal interest it has generated (Barry, 1973; Daniels, 1975) illustrate the intricacy of the problem. Inequality itself has not only been perplexing from a theoretical perspective, but it is of considerable practical importance. De Tocqueville's studies of early American democracy argue most forcefully for the superiority of egalitarian over hierarchical organization, e.g., colonial America versus eighteenth-century France. Subsequent empirical work has also focused on the trends of inequality within nations since the industrial revolution (Kuznets, 1955, 1963; Cutright, 1965, 1967; Paukert, 1973; Adelman and Morris, 1967, 1973; Chenery et al., 1974, 1975). The study of inequality within nations has begun to be set within a larger, global framework by such contemporary scholars as Galtung (1971), Chase-Dunn (1975), Rubinson (1976), and to a certain extent Jackman (1975). More recent theoretical and empirical work has suggested a "basic needs" perspective, which focuses upon the most essential needs (e.g., health, food, shelter, clothing) of the most disadvantaged portion of the population (Rawls, 1971; Galtung et al., 1975; Herrera et al., 1976). By virtually all accounts it has been established that inequality, along a wide variety of conceivable dimensions, is large within every nation in the world. The question of why is obviously important.

The second motivation is highly related to the first: inequality has been persistent within every country in the world, in spite of considerable attempts by certain groups and institutions to eliminate it, which, many would argue, have forced enduring attempts by others to maintain it. Like social cleavages (Lipset and Rokkan, 1967), inequalities within most nations appear to have changed very little within the past one-hundred and fifty years. A recent study reports that in France, where over one-hundred years ago a "successful" revolution sought to rectify pronounced inequalities, the total income of the upper ten percent of the population is roughly twenty times that of the lower ten percent (Sawyer, 1976). Not only has inequality everywhere been persistent, as well as resistant to any change, but also it has been argued to have a multitude of consequences within and outside of the polity. For example, it has been shown that, other things being equal, inequality leads to high levels of domestic political conflict (Gurr and Duvall, 1973). Russett (1964) studied the

[3]

relationship between land and income inequality and violent political deaths. It is often postulated that the level of support which a government receives is directly linked to the level of inequality (e.g., Mitchell, 1968; Nagel, 1974). Further, many authors have investigated the relationship between development, in the sense of industrialization and diversification, and the extent of inequality (e.g., Stallings, 1972; for a summary, Ranis, 1975; also Cline, 1975). Social stratification, in terms of status hierarchies, have also been theoretically linked to inequality and conflict by various authors (Coser, 1956; Dahrendorf, 1959; Lenski, 1966; Rummel, 1970). Finally, one ambitious study has investigated the level of inequality and its relationships with (1) democratic performance, (2) stability, (3) socialist orientation of labor unions and political parties, (4) violence, (5) cleavages, and (6) economic development and dependency (Jackman, 1975). Inequality is unquestionably important not only in respect to its purported causes, but also in terms of its potential consequences. These various studies have each addressed that essential question.

The third motivating factor is suggested by the first two. The extent, scope, and the persistence of inequality in virtually all countries provoke the notion that its recurrence is not merely coincidental. Rather, a structural approach seems a likely candidate to explain the persistence of this phenomenon. The search for the causes of inequality becomes a search for a structure that apparently reinforces the initially established patterns. The suggestion of a structural approach is predicated on the recurrence of patterns of inequality and, in part, by the notions offered for the importance of linking international and subnational phenomena.

The final motivation is simply the belief that inequality is in part caused by international factors, and that explanations which do not seek to explore these factors are inadequate. Moreover, virtually all of the recent issue themes of international affairs, from the cold war, environment, energy shortages, development, to dependency and its reversal, and the new economic order, all have strong undercurrents which are based upon deep and profound inequalities.

1.3 ORGANIZATION: DESIGN, DATA, AND PRESENTATION

The research design employed in this study is relatively straightforward. As a step toward eventual longitudinal and cross-level analysis, a recent time-slice was chosen, circa 1970. There is no question that there are problems with cross-sectional analysis in certain contexts (e.g., Moul, 1974). However, several reasons reinforce its use here. First, the data available to study inequality are, for the most part, cross-sectional. Very few data are available over a long time period which permit the investigation of inequality within a global perspective. Second, since inequalities have remained fairly resistant to marked temporal fluctuations, it does not appear that looking at a cross-section would grossly distort the longitudinal picture. More important is the fact that since they do not change over time, inequalities do not appear to be "caused" by the fluctuations in variables that do. It cannot be argued however, that they are unaffected by the confluence of fluctuations in other variables, but that, too, seems unlikely. The structural approach itself suggests that the most important question to be resolved deals not with what generates inequality, but rather concerns the preservation (i.e., reproduction) of the patterns which, for whatever reasons, do exist (e.g., Piaget, 1968). Thus, a structure itself may presumably be understood by cross-sectional analysis. Finally, the question of what accounts for the various differences in the levels of inequality within the nations of the globe is itself interesting, without regard to how inequality may be changing in any given nation over time. This research is undertaken as such a structural probe.

The countries selected for analysis include the largest polities from the 1970 era. Of the approximately 150 nation-states initially included in the study, severe missing data problems pruned the sample to 120. These countries are listed in Appendix A. Data were collected upon a host of pertinent variables for each of these 120 nations. The sources of that data, each variable's definition, and name(s) are reported in Appendix B.

A description of the organization of the study necessarily entails an outline of the remaining chapters. Since inequality was the central dependent variable to be explored, the research began with a collection of a new set of sectoral work force and gross domestic product data. *The World Handbook of Political and Social Indicators* (Taylor and Hudson, 1972), previously had collected Gini-type information based on similar data for about sixty polities in the early to mid 1960s. A new set of information on income inequality should not only expand the number of nations included, but also provide a temporal comparison to the earlier work. This task was undertaken and is reported in Chapter Two. Having completed that task, and obtained the resultant Gini scores, it became apparent that a more theoretically and empirically meaningful investigation should be undertaken with respect to the question of measuring inequality in contemporary polities. New data were collected, and new indices of inequality were constructed. These various measures were compared one to another, and a composite score was derived, which was the measure of inequality used throughout the remainder of the study. This new measure itself receives considerable attention in the bulk of Chapter Two. It should be noted that inequality is an independent as well as dependent variable in many contexts as well, although for the most part its role as a dependent variable constitutes the focus of this study.

Chapters Three and Four explore internal linkages to inequality. Initially, the previous work undertaken in economics by Kuznets (1955, 1963) and others was surveyed for its wisdom about the linkages between economic variables such as the level of development and the growth rate of an economy and the main dependent variable, inequality. A model was postulated which related each of these variables to inequality in an opposite fashion: growth was argued to aggravate inequality, while high levels of development were associated with lower levels of inequality. In Chapter Three, these arguments are examined with reference to the data set. Chapter Four adds the political components of policy effort in two major areas, education and unemployment, as additional determinants of lower levels of inequality. It was also argued that political mobilization of the masses was an important stimulus for higher levels of policy effort. These arguments were checked against the data via least-squares estimation.

Chapter Five constructs a theory of how the hierarchical structure of the international system impinges upon the internal determinants of inequality as well as the level of inequality itself. Specifically, it was posited that a hierarchy is a self-monitoring structure so that those low in the hierarchy have difficulty in translating increased economic and social product into greater levels of equality. These systemic constraints were posed in axiomatic and mathematical form. The latter specification of the theory was again examined by regression analysis. The last chapter summarizes the theoretical and empirical arguments and discusses some of their shortcomings and some of their implications.

REFERENCES

Adelman, I. and C. Morris (1967). Society, Politics, and Economic Development: A Quantitative Approach. Baltimore, Md.: Johns Hopkins Press.

Adelman, I. and C. Morris (1973). Economic Growth and Social Equity in Developing Countries. Stanford: Stanford University Press.

Allison, G. (1971). Essence of Decision: Explaining the Cuban Missile Crisis. Boston, Mass.: Little-Brown.

Barry, B. (1973). The Liberal Theory of Justice: A Critical Examination of the Principal Doctrines in 'A Theory of Justice' by John Rawls. Oxford: Clarendon Press.

Chase-Dunn, C. (1975). "The Effects of International Economic Dependence on Development and Inequality: A Cross-National Study." American Sociological Review, Vol. 40, pp 720-738.

Chenery, H., S. Ahluwalia, C. L. G. Bell, H. Duloy, and R. Jolly (1974). Redistribution with Growth. New York: Oxford University Press.

Chenery, H., M. Syrquin, with H. Elkington (1975). Patterns of Development, 1950-1970. New York: Oxford University Press.

Cutright, P. (1965). "Political Structure, Economic Development, and National Social Security Programs." American Journal of Sociology, Vol. 70, pp 537-550.

Cutright, P. (1967). "Inequality: A Cross-National Analysis." American Sociological Review, Vol. 32, pp 562-578.

Daniels, N. (1975). Reading Rawls: Critical Studies of 'A Theory of Justice'. New York: Basic Books.

Dos Santos, T. (1970). "The Structure of Dependence." American Economic Review, Vol. 60, No. 2, pp 231-236.

Duvall, R. (1975). International Stratification: Concept and Theory, unpublished PhD dissertation, Northwestern University.

Galtung, J. (1971). "A Structural Theory of Imperialism." Journal of Peace Research, Vol. 8, No. 2, pp 81-117.

Galtung, J., A. Guha, A. Wirak, S. Sjlie, M. Cifuentes, and H. Goldstein (1975). "Measuring World Development-I and II." Alternatives, Vol. 1, pp 131-158 and 523-555.

Gillespie, J. (1971). "Galton's Problem and Parameter Estimation Error in Comparative Political Analysis." Prepared for delivery at the Annual Meeting of the Midwest Political Science Association, Chicago, Ill.

Gurr, T., and R. Duvall (1973). "Civil Conflict in the 1960s: A Complete Theoretical System with Parameter Estimates." Comparative Political Studies, Vol. 6, No. 2, pp 135-169.

Jackman, R. (1975). Politics and Social Equality. New York: John Wiley.

Jencks, C., et al. (1972). Inequality: A Reassessment of the Effect of Family and Schooling in America. New York: Basic Books.

Herrera, A. O., H. D. Scolnik, et al. (1976). Catastrophe or New Society? A Latin American World Model. Ottawa: International Development Research Center.

Keohane, R. and J. Nye (1972). Transnational Relations and World Politics. Cambridge, Mass.: Harvard University Press.

Kravis, I. (1960). "International Differences in the Distribution of Income." Review of Economics and Statistics, Vol. 42, pp 408-416.

Kuznets, S. (1955). "Economic Growth and Income Inequality." American Economic Review, Vol. 45, pp 1-28.

Kuznets, S. (1963). "Quantitative Aspects of the Economic Growth of Nations, VIII: The Distribution of Income by Size." Economic Development and Cultural Change, Vol. 11, part 2 (entire).

Lenski, G. (1966). Power and Privilege: A Theory of Social Stratification. New York: McGraw-Hill.

Lipset, S. and S. Rokkan (1967). Party Systems and Voter Alignments: Cross-national Perspectives. New York: The Free Press.

Mitchell, E. J. (1968). "Inequality and Insurgency: A Statistical Study of South Vietnam." World Politics, Vol. 20, pp 421-438.

Moul, W. B. (1974). "On Getting Nothing for Something: A Note on Causal Models of Political Development." Comparative Political Studies, Vol. 7, No. 2, pp 139-164.

Nagel, J. (1974). "Inequality and Discontent: A Nonlinear Hypothesis." World Politics, Vol. 36, No. 4, pp 453-472.

Piaget, J. (1970). Structuralism. New York: Basic Books, translated by C. Maschler.

Ranis, G. (1975). "Equity and Growth." Journal of Conflict Resolution, Vol. 19, No. 3, pp 558-568.

Rawls, J. (1971). A Theory of Justice. Cambridge, Mass.: Harvard University Press.

Rubinson, R. (1976). "The World-Economy and the Distribution of Income within States: A Cross-National Study." American Sociological Review, Vol. 41, pp 638-659.

Russett, B. (1964). "Inequality and Instability: The Relation of Land Tenure to Politics." World Politics, Vol. 16, No. 3, pp 442-454.

Rosenau, J. (1969). Linkage Politics. New York: The Free Press.

Russo, A. (1972). "Economic and Social Correlates of Governmental Control in South Vietnam." Pp 314-324 in I.K. Feierabend, R.L. Feierabend, and T.R. Gurr, editors, Anger, Violence, and Politics. Englewood Cliffs, N.J.: Prentice-Hall.

Rummel, R. (1970). The Dimensions of Nations. Beverly Hills, California: Sage Publications.

Sawyer, M. (1976). OECD Study of Inequality discussed in Chicago Daily News, January 5, 1977, p. 5.

Taylor, C. and M. Hudson (1972). World Handbook of Political and Social Indicators, 2nd edition. New Haven, Conn.: Yale University Press.

Woodhouse, E. (1972). "Re-visioning the Future of the Third World: An Ecological Perspective on Development." World Politics, Vol 25, No. 1, pp 1-34.

[8]

Analyzing Societal Inequalities

2

2.1 INTRODUCTION

The distribution of valued objects and outcomes is an ancient problem that has increasingly commanded the attention of political scientists, economists, and sociologists in recent years. The study of inequality has accordingly spanned various substantive and theoretical subfields. Among the more recently visible endeavors has been the exciting work of Ramond Boudon (1974), who has examined mobility and education as they relate to inequality. The country-by-country study of the effects of income distribution upon economic development has produced a mountain of case studies concerned with economic inequality.[1] In a comparative framework, inequality has also been studied as a precondition or stimulant to violence (Gurr and Duvall, 1973). The recent "oil crises" have refocused attention on the questions of international inequalities by drawing attention to the shifting of investment capital out of the Western, industrial centers toward petroleum exporters (Akins, 1973). Moreover, the global modeling efforts of Herrera et al. (1976) and Tinbergen (1976) present the scholarly counterpart to the emerging of calls for a new international economic order in which the Third World nations share more equitably in the distribution of goods. In short, both empirical and theoretical studies have spread across virtually every level of analysis: city, state, country, and globe.

Societal inequalities, including aspects of wealth, education, and leisure, have been studied in a large number of ways. Alker (1965) provided one of the earliest surveys of measures for studying inequality. His attention focused upon variant approaches ranging from measures of dispersion to the well known Gini coefficient. Recent surveys (Ray and Singer, 1973) have been more extensive, inasmuch as they have explored many of the techniques developed by economists, demographers, and mathematical geographers.

However, several difficulties have confronted nearly all those concerned with the problem of inequality and the concomitant question of how to measure it. First, there is a relative paucity of data on the distribution of any valued good such as income, whether it is cross-sectional or longitudinal. Consider then theories that attempt to explore the distributions of several values—say income, educational opportunities, and public services. The data problems are staggering, although there is mounting evidence (e.g., Chenery et al., 1974) that these problems are diminishing through collaborative efforts. Second, relative to the attention they are given, few convincing substantive findings have been accumulated by these many studies. Most analyses have been plagued by a relatively high ratio of missing information, thus potentially biasing the results. Moreover, longitudinal data have been extremely difficult to obtain.

Third, while there has been much attention devoted to how to measure inequality, much of this activity has been undertaken without explicit concern for compatibility, replicability, and cumulation. That is, few researchers concerned with how best to measure inequality have actually compared either their theoretical or empirical solutions to other proposed methods via empirical data. One notable exception is the early work of Alker and Russett (1966), which compared five measures of inequality of representation for twenty-seven state senates. The general insularity of these many efforts has had another, perhaps more important consequence. Namely, social scientists have little experience with how to measure, and thereby how to interpret, this concept of inequality which is so central to many social science theories. The centrality of this concept is well underscored by Gurr (forthcoming), who notes, that "every inherited or acquired trait by which human groups are distinguishable has been occasion for vicious distinctions in the allocation of goods."

This chapter conceptually and empirically surveys several of the important strategies for measuring inequality. In addition to the extant strategies identified, several additional ones are developed. The domestic inequalities of 120 contemporary polities are the primary body of referent data utilized in the empirical comparisons.

The first basic task accomplished in this chapter is initially to review some of the uses of the concept of inequality in several relevant disciplines, highlighting those prominent in political science. This provides a context in which inequality is typically used by scholars and policy makers, as well as illustrations of the grammar which researchers frequently employ in order to construct meaningful scientific statements within that context. Also, it allows the examination of divergent conceptual and definitional lines of argument developed in the explication of the concept by other scholars in any one of several disciplines, e.g., psychology, sociology, economics, and political science.

Competing explanatory frameworks have developed. These are explored, spanning the conservative, (neo)classical economic perspective, and the liberal work of Rawls (1971), and the (neo)Marxian framework typified by Galtung (1974), *inter alios*. Brief surveys are undertaken since each separate thrust has unique implications for the conceptualization and measurement of inequality.

Until recently, many scholars exhibited remarkable similarity in their conceptualizations of inequality. Generally, the notion has been used to refer to the idea that roughly equal units should receive roughly equal treatment. With this definition of inequality linked to the scholarly literature of several disciplines, the operational stage is explored.

Unlike the relative conceptual convergence, vast differences of opinion exist on how exactly to measure this concept. Further, since the most conventional measure, the Gini index, is shown to have several operational flaws, new measures are also suggested. The most distinctive is a conceptual mapping rule conceived simply as a ratio of the gross level of poverty to the gross level of affluence in a social unit. The justification of this index is also simple: if there is a great deal of both poverty and affluence, then there is also inequality.

This "conceptual map" is used to measure the level of inequality in 120 contemporary nations. The results are compared with five other measurement strategies: (1) Gurr's extension of the Adelman and Morris scale of social immobility; (2) Hibbs' summated Z-score measure; (3) a sector based Gini index; (4) an individual level Gini index; and (5) a measure of the relative dispersion of telephone services within the polity. From this set of variables, a summary index is constructed.

2.2 CONCEPTUAL FOUNDATIONS AND EMPIRICAL EVIDENCE

As noted earlier, many researchers of the inequality question have roughly similar ideas of what is meant by the term 'equality'. Furthermore, the notions of what is therefore meant by inequality are also widely shared. Unfortunately, a survey of relevant works has revealed very few formal definitions of either concept. Of the remaining informal, implied definitions, virtually all share as their nexus the idea that roughly equal units defined in terms of size, rights, or some other delineating characteristic, share roughly equally in the available resources of the social system.

Juxtaposed with such naturalist perspectives are two related but distinct traditions. One is the utilitarian perspective, and the other the relatively recent Rawlsian view of inequality. While Plato and many later naturalists felt that inequalities emerge as a result of certain "natural" causes such as beauty, intelligence, and strength, and further that social contracts were primarily undertaken to control the influence of these natural forces, both the utilitarian and the Rawlsian perspective identify inequalities which emerge precisely from those social institutions and rules which govern man's activities. The utilitarian desire for redress of these inequalities is aimed at increasing what is perceived to be the greater good. Rawls, on the other hand, desires the amelioration of inequalities so as to benefit the most-disadvantaged members of society, rather than the collectivity. A neo-Marxist viewpoint is present in the writings of Galtung (1974), in which inequality is viewed to have two important aspects: (1) the potential reality of equality, and (2) the empirical reality of equality. Two areas are proposed as arenas for assessing these potentialities and realities. At one level, it means equality of ownership, while at another level it means an equal share in decision making activity.

What becomes apparent almost immediately is that there is virtually no difference in any of the implied definitions of inequality offered by these four lines of thought. Plato, Bentham, Hobbes, Rawls, and Galtung all agree, at least as simplistically presented here, on the definition of equality: roughly, it means equal ownership of social goods, one of which is access to the allocative decision process by roughly equal entities. What they differ on is not the definition but

[12]

rather the causes, consequences, particularly the normative ones, and potential remedies for this condition.

From Adam Smith to the present, economists have studied the area of inequality, rarely giving explicit attention to definitional questions. For example, one of the most thoroughly comparative investigations (Chiswick, 1974) does not give any attention to the definitional questions. The World Bank sponsored work of Chenery and associates (1974,1975) also is not concerned with defining inequality. This is understandable from an economic standpoint, since the unstated definition, that the economic product is widely distributed across all strata of society, is readily interpretable in terms of "well-developed" theory about the determinants of individual and factor income. Thus, once the appropriate adjustments are made (i.e., adjustments of raw income to operationalized, refining theoretical statements), it simply remains to examine whether or not there is any marked concentration of product across social and economic units. Such a strategy has focused economic studies on national product and its individual counterparts. A most interesting simulation study based upon a hypothetical system of one-hundred wage earners and their families through some seven generations is presented in Pryor (1971). Ramond Boudon (1974) has also used simulations to study patterns of mobility and inequality *vis-a-vis* educational opportunity.

Recently, however, there have been several stringent critiques of this approach (Galtung, 1974; Tobin and Nordhaus, 1972), which generally have been directed toward the creation of indicators of the quality of life rather than the general level of economic well being represented by GNP and personal income measures. Sociologists and social psychologists have been somewhat more concerned with definitional problems.

Several of these critiques are couched in terms of basic needs. There are two facets to such approaches. First, there exists the notion that not income, but rather the provision of human needs such as clothing, shelter, and food is more desirable in the short run than abstract levels of equality. Moreover, these needs are more likely to be directly manipulable via social policy. Second, there is the idea, following Rawls, that:

Social and economic inequalities are to be arranged so that they are both: (a) to the greatest benefit of the least advantaged ... and (b) attached to offices

[13]

and positions open to all under the condition of fair equality of opportunity [1971:302].

Since the analysis undertaken here does not assume that there exists a "magic number" allowing the categorical comparison of inequality in different settings, and since the basic needs arguments are suggested, a host of social goods are examined. Galtung et al. (1975) have suggested that basic needs such as food, clothing, shelter, leisure time, as well as income, job opportunities, and the like should constitute at least one focus of inequality research, under the rubric of World Social Goals. Currently, there is insufficient data on most of these dimensions on which to base wide ranging comparative analysis, as undertaken here.

Interest in the basic needs approach is growing, however. Both the International Labour Office (ILO) and the Overseas Development Council (ODC) have been active in promoting these interests. A recent ILO volume (1977) surveys the activities in this field and addresses the "State of the Globe" in regard to the provision of basic needs. Two recent studies of the Global Condition, each related to the Club of Rome efforts and stimulus, have directed some attention to the basic needs strategy for improving the level of equality in the world. James Grant and Mahbub ul Haq, working with the ILO and the ODC, were instrumental in the inclusion of a basic needs perspective in the work led by Nobel Laureate Jan Tinbergen, *RIO: Reshaping the International Order*. Moreover, the Latin American World Model, constructed under the direction of Amilcar Herrera and Hugo Scolnik, paid considerable attention to the distribution of basic needs, as embodied in the notion of optimizing life expectancy at birth, as it reflects both health and wealth.

It would be well to include explicit basic needs measures in this study, but as mentioned no large body of comparable data exists as yet. However, this study focuses on more than income statistics. In addition to income statistics, it probes infant mortality, provision of health care, nutritional standards, preventable disease such as typhoid, motor vehicle fatalities, and many other measures of the distribution of various social goods/values/outcomes. Thus, it seems appropriate to note the emphasis placed upon the analysis of societal inequality, as opposed to income inequality, in this endeavor. Moreover, indicators of the basic needs *genre* are examined where possible, and the research strategy explicitly seeks to avoid complete reliance upon financial data.

[14]

It is to be hoped that in the efforts to come, more comparisons can be made among more direct measures of basic needs, the mixture of societal inequalities proposed here, and the more conventional analysis of income inequality *per se*. It should be noted, however, that the flourishing of basic needs suggestions has not yet blossomed into a wealth of empirical studies. More interesting is the recent imbroglio about the utility of a basic needs oriented theory of, among other things, foreign aid. The basic needs perspective has gained considerable popularity in the industrialized countries and institutions of the North, where, incidentally, it is used as an argument for smaller as opposed to larger aid transfers and loans to the developing economies of the South. The view from the South has not been particularly supportive in this strategy for development aid. Some less developed countries (LDC) have "disputed the notion that raising the living standards of their impoverished population and not piling up showy economic statistics is the ultimate goal of development policy" (Tonelson, 1977:1). The basic division rests upon a perception of who is to blame for current global and domestic inequalities. Industrial countries have desired a new focus on equity, not growth. LDCs have argued for increased growth as a solution to the equity problem. In the words of one Third World diplomat, the basic needs perspective of the industrial North has at its root "the desire to perpetuate neocolonial dependence to direct international cooperation towards partial goals and to mask the effects of underdevelopment instead of attacking its deeper cures" (Tonelson, 1977:1).

Generally, inequality has been discussed in terms of stratification theory. Thus, inequality has status as its primary sociological referent or backdrop. Often income serves as a surrogate for this status backdrop. Sociologically then, the primary question has been: Are social (sub)units stratified? To the extent that they are, they exhibit inequality. Political scientists have not differed greatly from the sister-disciplines, yet one main theoretical underpinning in this discipline, not characteristic in others, has been the possession of explicitly political goods, such as the right to vote. There has been an expansion of this notion by those concerned with the relationship between inequality and development: ". . . to see a more nearly complete picture and to make more highly discriminant judgments, anyone who is concerned with political development in any way involving measurement or comparisons should take full account of some of the measurable elements of the political goods of security, justice,

[15]

liberty, and welfare" (Pennock, 1966:434). This definition is similar to the one which Duvall, in one of the most formalized definitional treatments, expands: ". . . social inequality is the extent of differences in the possession or realization of social goods by social entities" (1975:8).[2]

These formulations tend to follow the tradition of earlier scholars in that (in Duvall's terms) the definitional question of "the extent of differences" is left to measurement strategies.

One area not explicitly mentioned by many researchers is the precise list of social goods that should be examined. Often a partial vague list is offered and then one is chosen for further exploration and analysis. This approach is the classic one of economists who typically study income inequality. This is partly justified on the basis of extant economic theory, but unfortunately, other social scientists have not advanced much beyond this primarily economic type analysis. Duvall's work points out the theoretical difficulties with this type of single good approach. Theories of inequality must deal with a multitude of social goods allocated by the political system. Barber's recent criticism (1975) of Rawls' work also notes this problem from a measurement perspective. Basically, the problem is that income, which is the most frequently proffered candidate, is quite problematic. As Barber notes, in the U.S. the division of the population into "blacks, white middle-class students, women, the rural poor, blue-collar workers, and ... the middle class" (1975:677) presents several dimensions of the allocation of social goods more salient than income alone. Consequently, one reasonable requirement of measures of inequality is the ability to deal with a multitude of salient social goods.

That the "extent of differences" is left to operational terms in all of the disciplines discussed above is indicative of what these various perspectives and conceptualizations share most of all: inequality as an outcome of power relationships.

Sociological studies have implicitly utilized a power/stratification formulation. For example, the experimental work of Cook (1975) has shown that if rank expectations are well-formed, then if there is a violation of expectations (i.e., the unequal exchange model), the individual will at the first chance given attempt to adjust these outcomes of the exchange relationships (i.e., the inequalities). Further, it was discovered that when no rank expectations are held, there is a greater tolerance of inequality. This stands in direct contradiction to the experimental work of Morgan and Sawyer (1967). The conceptualization of inequalities in terms of the unequal exchange (differential conversion) of energy is also implicit in the works of the economists—especially the work of Emmanual (1972). Elliot provides one of the most fascinating explications:

> ... [T]he major outline of the system: It comprises a set of goldfish bowls, set one on top of another. Each is smaller than the one beneath it, but the fish it contains are larger, although less numerous. Now these bowls are connected by means of access cones, so that a determined or lucky fish can pass from a lower bowl to a higher one. These cones vary in shape, diameter, and position within the bowl. At the simplest, the cone is little more than a cylinder set in the bottom of the bowl. The fish can see clearly the size of the further orifice, the length of the cone, and the feasibility of passing up it. But some cones are set on the convex side of the bowl and may thus give an illusion with respect to the real nature of the cone—its size, its length, and the difficulty involved in getting up it ... [M]ost fish in fact wish to pass into a higher bowl; competition on these access cones is therefore intense...There is a further feature of these cones: They change over time...as a direct result of the pressure on them from below, expanding to meet at least some of the excessive demand for access.... The conical character of these access routes ... implies that it is unusual for a fish to make the reverse passage down the system [1975:4].

In fact, one of the few findings which has cumulated within and across disciplinary boundaries utilizes this type of framework. To be explicit, much work has shown that the access to educational resources is among the strongest covariants of unequal distributions of economic welfare. Chiswick (1974) has shown that "returns" to schooling, measured in terms of school enrollment ratios, are highly related to the differential shares of income held by the top, middle, and lower income groups. In a sociological study, Schiller noted:

> The weight of accumulated evidence thus firmly supports the stratified opportunity hypothesis. What we have observed is that there are tremendous achievement disparities between AFDC and non-AFDC youth...these disparities cannot be explained on the basis of parental or occupational statuses [1970;439].

Much work in political science has also been done within a power oriented model. For example, in a series of heated debates in *World Politics* during the last six years, several scholars argued over the relationship between governmental political and military control and inequality in South Vietnam.[3] Russett (1964) investigated the relation-

[17]

ship between inequality and instability and found that the extent of land inequality in a polity was moderately related (r = .45) to the level of domestic instability. Thus, he argued:

> Tocqueville's basic observation would therefore appear correct: no state can long maintain a democratic form of government if the major sources of economic gain are divided very unequally among its citizens [1964:453].

Gurr, in similar vein, has emphasized both the attitudinal (1970) and structural (1973) components of conflict. In this light, his primary conclusion is that "invidious" discrepancies in the ways in which political, social, and economic values are distributed in society are the most important determinants of mass political conflict. It is hardly surprising that all of these works share control or allocation as their implicit, primary background.

2.3 CONCEPTUAL AND METHODOLOGICAL ANALYSIS

One of the difficulties which has tended to militate against the cumulation of findings about inequality has been the lack of sufficient attention to both the analytics and empirics of measurement. This section will review the major operational definitions that have been suggested by scholars to measure inequality. This task is not undertaken merely to recatalogue the summaries already compiled by Ray and Singer (1973) and Taussig (1973); rather, it seeks to broaden the framework for measuring inequalities by pointing out the narrowness with which scholars have typically attacked this problem.

2.31 Gini Index and the Lorenz Curve. Corrado Gini (1936) suggested a measure of inequality which has gained great popularity among modern social scientists. This coefficient is based upon a very rich conceptual model of equality. The assumptions are simple yet strong. Basically, this model presumes that every social or organizational unit in any given system should possess equal amounts of valued objects/outcomes/goods. That is, for every N social units, each such unit should possess 1/Nth of the total value allocated among system members. Quite simply, one person, one vote. Virtually all other measures embody this premise in one form or another. Inequality becomes, then, any set of distributions that does not satisfy the equal

[18]

FIGURE 2.1. The Lorenz Curve and Inequality

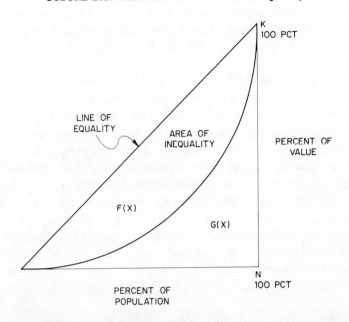

share principle. This condition is very simple to operationalize and test. However, this sort of testing only yields a two-state information return: either there is inequality or there is equality.

It is important to understand more about the degrees of inequality, since virtually every valued object/ouctome/good is unequally distributed. Gini's initial suggestion was that a monotonic, cumulative density curve be compared mathematically with a curve representing the condition of equality. By specifying monotonicity of the density function, one requires that the social units be ordered before cumulation relative to the amount of value each possesses. Hence, the resultant curve becomes monotonic over the cumulative proportions of both value and units. The greater the area between this density function (g(x)) and the line of equality (f(x)), the greater, Gini argued, the inequality in the distribution of values. Mathematically this is represented as:

(2.1)   Gini = $2 \int f(x) - g(x) \, dx$.

Figure 2.1 presents an example of these two curves, and also pictorially interprets this conceptualization and measurement of inequality.

The Gini index ranges from 0.0 to 1.0, and increments in its value represent a larger amount (area) of inequality. Thus a situation of perfect equality has a Gini score of 0.0, while a value of 1.0 represents the situation wherein 1/Nth of the population possesses 100 percent of the total value.

The attractiveness of this index for social scientists has been considerable, perhaps because it is conceptually isomorphic to many notions of what is meant by inequality. The mathematical elegance of the simple formulation corresponds with the way in which many think of inequality: in comparison with a perfectly equal situation. This index comes close to what many might argue as the ideal in measurement: a concept is isolated, analytics are developed to formalize that concept, and finally, the operationalization proceeds in a simple fashion, presumably very close to the pure analytic formulation. Having defined inequality and its measurement in the terms suggested by Gini, one can quite simply "go out" to the referent system and survey social units to discover the amount of value that each of them possesses (i.e., What is your family income?). From this information, a Gini coefficient can be computed.[4]

Despite the conceptual elegance of Gini's seminal formulation, this index is not without its difficulties. As has been pointed out, although it has been used as the primary measure of inequality, very little knowledge has accumulated about the causes of inequality so measured. This criticism is not necessarily a devastating one, for a multitude of extremely plausible explanations for this situation can easily be offered: inappropriate design, unimaginative investigation, bad data, and most importantly perhaps, the lack of appropriate theory. Yet, each of these in itself is unsatisfactory.

Like most measures of overall patterns, the Gini index also suffers from a certain amount of instability if only a few cases are used (i.e., in small systems) in its calculations. More importantly, it has been noted (Ray and Singer, 1973; Duvall, 1975) that it does not give a unique score value for differently unequal conditions. That is, there are many ways for a social system to have distributed value X over N units such that Gini is equal to some constant value A.[5]

A more constricting problem is data related. For many purposes, insufficient data are collected for calculating this index. The seminal work of Simon Kuznets (1963) is illustrative of this problem and has provided a type of solution for estimating the inequality of wealth within nations. Kuznets was faced with the problem of calculating a Gini score for many nations for which there were no data on the individual (or family) income shares. His solution was to utilize the eight sectors of the economy to approximate individual level data. This approximation, Kuznets argued, reflects the average product generated per worker within each sector. It simply assumes that each sector is roughly equally "efficient" in producing income from human labor, a somewhat questionable assumption, though it has been accepted by many as a reasonable approximation of income distribution in nations. However, it does tend to underestimate the income inequality by assuming that there is no inequality of income within any one sector.

This ingenious technique suggested by Kuznets has been used by most cross-sectional analysts of national inequality. First, one must collect data on the percentage of the work force employed in each sector of the economy as well as how much of the total gross domestic product (GDP) is generated within any given sector. Then, sectors are sorted from low to high (or high to low), based upon the ratio of the percent of the total work force to percent of GDP generated in any sector. This sorting operation insures that the cumulative density function, or Lorenz curve, be monotone on both axes. The Gini index for any given country is then calculated by integrating the area between the line of perfect equality and the Lorenz curve.

Kuznets (1963), as well as Taylor and Hudson (1972), point out that the comparison between different cases does not take into account such structural variables as the level of wealth or income. One important bias in this approximation derives from the division of many developing countries into urban-industrial, and therefore densely populated, and rural-agrarian, but often sparsely populated, areas. An example of this may be seen in the case of Thailand. The urban population generates most of the wealth in Thailand, since the population in the other areas is largely involved in subsistence farming. This does not mean that there are no urban poor. The influence of these divisions tends to distort the picture of inequality given by the Gini measure by assuming that the number of workers engaged in a particular set of economic activities such as manufacturing is directly and linearly related to their productivity in terms of national product.

Work by Chintakananda (1976) can be used to illustrate this aggregation bias. Chintakananda surveyed approximately three-thousand family units in Thailand in early 1970 for information on their spending and savings patterns. Each family kept detailed records on their money and barter transactions for a period of one calendar month. From these data, Gini indices were constructed for both the urban (i.e., municipal) and rural families in each of the five administrative regions in Thailand. The results are presented in Table 2.1. Though Chintakananda's work does not suffer from the problem of assuming that inequality is nonexistent within any unit, the differences both between rural and urban family income as well as the pockets of inequality in the Northeast, where much of the wealth is concentrated, clearly demonstrates that such an assumption is untenable and would understate the actual aggregate inequality.[6] Many developing societies have labor intensive, agricultural sectors as well as capital intensive, industrial sectors which often grow at rapid rates. Sector based Gini scores will mostly underestimate the level of actual inequality in such situations. More properly, Kuznets' approximation is very sensitive to the relative balance of the economy *vis-a-vis* the largest sectors which are usually agricultural and manufacturing, given the fact that the characteristic balance often corresponds with two other reinforcing, distinguishing attributes: urban *versus* rural, and densely *versus* sparsely populated urban regions.

There are several other Gini type measures which have been used to

TABLE 2.1. *Inequality of Family Income in Thailand (1972)**

| | GINI SCORES (Unadjusted) | | | |
| | Municipal | | Rural | |
REGION	FAMILIES	INDIVIDUALS	FAMILIES	INDIVIDUALS
North	0.45	0.67	0.41	0.70
Central	0.44	0.65	0.44	0.72
Northeast	0.51	0.69	0.44	0.72
South	0.46	0.61	0.39	0.70
Capital	0.42	0.64	0.40	0.65
Overall	0.45	0.55	0.50	0.78

*Data provided by Chintakananda through personal communication.

[22]

describe income inequality by social scientists. Of these the most prominent is the Schutz coefficient. Jackman (1975) has used this index to measure the actual policy impact of social welfare programs upon the distribution of the income.[7] The index is calculated by accumulating the difference in slopes between the line of equality and the Lorenz curve over the interval from 0.0 to where the slope of the Lorenz curve is at the fair share point (i.e., where the slope of the Lorenz curve is 1.0). It can be demonstrated that this is a fairly straightforward transformation of the Gini index, since the cumulation of the difference in slopes for the case of sectors is equivalent to Schutz coefficient. When Alker and Russett examined the correlation between the Gini and Schutz coefficients in twenty-seven state senates measured on representativeness, the correlation was found to be perfect. Because of this redundancy, the Schutz coefficient has been excluded from further consideration in this study.[8]

In summary, the Gini index is conceptually and analytically a rich measure. The attractiveness which it holds for scholars concerned with inequality continues unabated.

2.32 *Substantively Based Conceptual Additions.* In many respects these theoretical, analytical approaches to the measurement of inequality reflect highly abstract strategies which can be applied across a broad range of substantive areas. For example, Duvall (1975) holds the substance of his study (stratification in the international system) in abeyance until he develops the conceptual formulations of inequality as well as measurement strategies. In contrast to such approaches, several scholars have developed indicators of inequality which have been more directly related to their particular substantive domains of inquiry.

Phillips Cutright (1967) was among the first to examine inequality in this fashion. He was investigating the relationship betweeen economic development and social security programs for communist and noncommunist nations, utilizing data gathered by the U.S. Social Security Administration. There are five types of social security programs according to the classification systems of the Social Security Administration: work-injury programs; sickness programs; old-age programs; family allowance programs; and unemployment insurance programs. Cutright found that these five types of programs (plus the category of no program) form a six-item Guttman scale of increasing difficulty with a reproducibility of over 0.96. Substantively, this means that a country with an unemployment insurance program is likely to have each of the other programs. If a nation has family allowance programs, but no unemployment program, it is likely to have the other programs appearing before it in the above list.

Jackman (1975) expanded Cutright's original notions to include experience with, or age of, social insurance programs. His policy related index is based upon the sum of the number of years each existing program has been in operation. A country that has operated all five programs for a long period of time will have a high score on the Jackman index, while countries with only a few or recently formed programs will receive a low score. More precisely, this index is a measure of the policy effort which is directed at redistribution and will therefore be dropped as a measure of inequality *per se*.

Further, following Hibbs (1973), Jackman constructed a summated standard score (henceforth called Z-scores) index using physicians *per* million inhabitants; live birth *per* 1,000 births *per annum*; caloric consumption *per capita per diem*; and, protein consumption *per capita per diem*. The summation of Z-scores accomplishes several goals. First, it embodies the convergent strategy of multiple operationalism. Second, the technique maximizes the available data for each case.[9] Finally, each component is scaled and weighted equally. Consequently, none of the Z-score components can easily distort the overall value of the index. Since these particular four values cannot reasonably be held by a small elite portion of the population, their summation is said to reflect their distribution. Thus, a high score is held to represent a distribution of great equality, while a low score reflects a nonegalitarian distribution. Jackman (1975) notes a partial corroboration of this argument based upon the work of Tord Hoivik (1971), which shows a positive relationship between social inequality in income and nutritional and health benefits.

Gurr (1970) and Gurr and Duvall (1973) have also utilized a similar approach in their work. One of the major determinants of domestic political conflict in their models is internal political strain. A primary indicator of strain is the proportion of the population facing overt (economic, social, and/or political) discrimination. Gurr (forthcoming) argues against the use of income inequality measures like Gini, because in addition to the paucity of data there are "wide differences in cultural norms about how much, or little, inequality is justifiable."

[24]

While hardly an analytic criticism of these measures *per se,* this decision does reflect concern over the difficulty in accurately assessing inequality in an empirical fashion. Consequently, Gurr has defined discrimination as systematic exclusion of social groups from some sought after good, i.e., political participation and economic goods. Based upon earlier work (1966, 1968), he has coded eighty-six polities upon these two variables. Gurr has also expanded the work of Adelman and Morris (1973) by coding polities on a social immobility index. This indicator is based upon the interaction of three variables: (1) the size of the middle class as defined by the International Labour Organisation (i.e., clerical, administrative, technical, commercial, and professional occupation groupings), (2) extent of education, and, (3) the level of group discrimination, as defined above.

Another example of a similar approach is found in Chenery's work (1974) for the World Bank. Chenery and associates have been studying the income distributions in nations with developing economies. The two indicators chosen are the income share of the lowest forty percent and the top twenty percent of the population. With this approach, the measurement of equality is attempted through several means. Thus, few empirical studies have demonstrated a great deal of faith in any one measure. There are many ways to approach the dictum of Kelvin, and it would seem that the metric of inequality is still open to investigation.

Taylor and Hudson report one promising attempt to develop a measure of inequality which is potentially more easily and directly operationalized than Gini based measures. Succinctly, that strategy lies in attempting to measure both poverty and affluence for a given social unit. The ratio of poverty to affluence should be indicative of the distribution of wealth. Thus, "[f]or example, when indicators of affluence are relatively high but indicators of basic needs are relatively low, there is probably maldistribution of income" (Taylor and Hudson, 1972:214). Reported analysis for Western Europe shows a high correspondence between these efforts and the Gini index.[10] Yet few reports have surfaced on this research by United Nations Institute for Social Development (Drewnoski and Scott, 1966). Further, the Western European nations do not present a wide enough range of variation in income inequality to suggest with confidence that they generate findings applicable to developing countries.

Although apparently not yet utilized, it would seem that this simple ratio strategy has enormous potential in the measurement of national inequalities. First, most other measures are practically, though not conceptually, restricted to income based inequality. That is, about the only value on which there is abundant and robust data is income—yet even these data are woefully inadequate and incomplete.

Kuznets' formulation can be extended to other values, but only in a very troublesome fashion. This is primarily true for a set of reinforcing reasons. First, the theories of economics are somewhat well developed with respect to individual income and its aggregation into national product—though they are by no means complete. Thus, the conceptual leaps made by Kuznets are somewhat justified upon theoretical grounds. Second, because of this robustness, relatively good data is collected on the income of individuals and nations. Virtually every survey conducted will ask family income as a matter of course. Inequality can often be gauged by piecing together information from social surveys. None of these conditions is as true for the other objects/values distributed by the social system. The industry of Chenery and associates (1974,1975) should serve as proof that such a "data grubbing" strategy is potentially very fruitful. More importantly, by assembling machine-readable survey responses as well as culling the journalistic and academic tomes for information, it may soon be possible to begin to assess the patterns of inequality of education, shelter, leisure time, and other values that are related to income but are by no means isomorphic to it.

There are three major advantages to this approach. First, inequality analysis can be extended beyond the bounds of economics and its mainstay, income. Scholars can begin to analyze the other multigood domains of inequality as well. Though this has long been recognized as important, for a host of reasons little has yet been done. Second, this strategy is a hands-on approach which should allow some experimentation with the precise form of measurement techniques, given the limitations of the data. This is an opportunity not easily afforded by Gini-based measures, although it is possible to modify Gini-type measures based upon a reconceptualization of what equality is. For example, one might argue that there is some additional factor, based on the accumulation of capital. Thus, the more one has, the more one tends to accumulate. From this we might argue that there is not a constant return to scale for equality conditions. Accordingly, the line of perfect equality should not necessarily be linear. Thus, a new Gini measure would ensue. Since the linearity is supplied either theoretically or empirically by the researcher, it may be modified in light of his needs and findings. It is exceedingly important to note that this sort of modification does not alleviate many of the problems exhibited by this type of index. This is not intended to suggest, however, that social scientists only seek face validity and leave in abeyance the theoretical questions involved in index construction.

Although many of the aspects of inequality will not be easily operationalized in the foreseeable future, they are nevertheless important for many reasons: completeness, heuristic relevance, but most importantly because of the deductions and inferences which may be drawn from the juxtaposition of these and other conceptual arguments.

It is exceedingly unlikely, if not impossible, that the potential, resultant insights could be obtained if the conceptual domain were unrealistically constrained by the strict criterion of measurability. The deduction which may be drawn from a domain including easily measured concepts as well as those for which data are likely to remain unavailable for some time to come may themselves include only easily measurable concepts, and thus may be "readily" subjected to empirical evaluation. Third, there exists sufficient data for this type of middle-range strategy to be immediately useful. Additionally, there is nothing sacrosanct about Gini type measures. Given our skills and opportunities for observation (i.e., measurement), and the consequently poor quality of the data with which we often work, it is possible that the more simplistic and less mathematically demanding assumptions might prove a viable interim alternative to the Gini measures of inequality.

A society with a low degree of both affluence and poverty is said to be a relatively equal society. It must be remembered that this section refers only to the aggregate level of poverty and affluence, not the relative affluence or poverty of an individual. This relative equality is the result of the condition of no apparent maldistribution of either wealth or poverty. The basic premise of the ratio strategy is presented in Table 2.2. As stated, this is neither analytically nor empirically valid. However, it does represent a "reasonable" guess as to the characteristics of a distribution given these conditions. It is quite possible for a society's affluence to be concentrated in a few hands and its poverty concentrated elsewhere. Throughout all of this analysis we make no distinction between public and private goods. Thus, the distribution is fairly "unequal."

Nonetheless, it seems more likely that if there is a low level of both

TABLE **2.2.** *Inferring Inequality from Dichotomous Information on Poverty and Affluence in Social Units*

	INEQUALITY SCORES Extent of Poverty	
Extent of Affluence	LOW	HIGH
Low	1	3
High	2	4

Range of inequality score (1,4)

poverty and affluence the society has distributed some values in a relatively equal manner. That is, there are no great extremes. The case of high poverty and high affluence is a similar one. Thus, it is argued that it is relatively impossible for a society with both great affluence and great poverty to have a relatively equal distribution of both these conditions across its members. There is a high probability that such a society will be characterized by high inequality. Even though these two "pure" cases are not really pure, because they involve a substantial leap of faith, the contention made here seems plausible. More importantly, it is open to empirical examination.

The two mixed cases are not so "straightforward," inasmuch as we face the problem of ordering them not relative to the extremes but relative to each other. Does a society with high affluence and low poverty tend to be more unequal than one with low affluence and high poverty? The answer to this question is difficult to formulate without making additional assumptions about inequality and/or societies in general. This has been approached in the following way: it is assumed that affluence tends to influence the level of inequality more strongly than does poverty. This assumption is based on the knowledge that the richest segments in societies tend to be relatively smaller in absolute numbers than the poorest segments. Again this qualifying assumption is somewhat tenuous though explicit; consequently, high affluence and low poverty conditions are ranked as more unequal than the inverse.[11]

Two auxiliary axioms are introduced to classify cases within the range of all possible mixtures of poverty and affluence. The first is that affluence is more important in determining the level of inequality in a social unit than is poverty. Thus, for two societies with equal levels of poverty, the one with the greater level of affluence exhibits more

[28]

inequality. The second is that for societies that have rough parity between poverty and affluence, the inequality is directly related to the level of both poverty and wealth.

This strategy is not limited to the case of dichotomizing information, and it has been extended to the polychotomous case in Table 2.3. Thus, the existence of distinguishable levels of poverty and affluence is posited. From that assumption the above conceptual map is deduced. Three points are worth stressing. This strategy is eminently flexible and is easily modified by those not accepting the explicit enabling assumptions. It is a new cut at the difficult task of measuring inequality, and one which is relatively easily constructed. It is a relative indicator, not an absolute one. That is, it allows comparisons across cases rather than to an abstract ideal level of "perfect equality," as in the case of the Gini index. Further, the prepared measure can be adapted to a more normative perspective by specifying acceptable levels of poverty and affluence.

Having established this conceptual map, one needs to choose appropriate indicators and cutting points for both poverty and affluence. A strategy of this sort has a myriad of advantages and disadvantages. On the positive side, researchers can utilize this plan to study the ratio of the general level of affluence to poverty by composite indices produced theoretically and based upon some scaling of available data as well as the ratio of some specific domain of inequality such as wealth, education, or employment. Further, there are a lot of data on these types of social indicators. Such an approach will also allow a

TABLE 2.3. *Inferring Inequality from Polychotomous Information on Poverty and Affluence in Social Units*

	INEQUALITY SCORES Extent of Poverty		
Extent of Affluence	LOW (1)	HIGH (2)	EXTREME (3)
Low (1)	1	3	5
High (2)	2	6	8
Extreme (3)	4	7	9

Range of inequality score (1,9)

[29]

great deal of theoretical and empirical flexibility to remain at the discretion of the researcher. Moreover, the index produced contains no assumption about the intervals between different scores; rather, it is an ordinal measure. Further, it leaves to empirical tasks the explicit discovery of appropriate metrics. This strategy does share with most others a host of typical measurement problems, most notably reliability.

The substitution of a new approximation which is based upon the relative balance of affluence and wealth for an income-based measure of inequality, gives rise to a new crop of conceptual and operational difficulties, which, however, are not entirely intractable. How exactly does one derive the exact ratio? What form will it take? Should it be based on a simple or absolute difference, or should an actual ratio be formed? Will multivariate techniques such as multidimensional scaling be useful? Furthermore, are we only interested in the total balance across a set of dimensions such as food, clothing, shelter, education, and leisure? Or is it important to keep the disaggregations and derive a set of inequality scores for each of these domains as well as for their composite? Also, exactly how should we construct the composite? Depending upon the set of answers to these typical measurement questions, the complexity of the task may increase exponentially. In the following section the precise procedures employed in this study are outlined. Irrespective of the answers provided below, it is hoped that the strategy outlined above will be useful to other researchers.

2.4 OPERATIONAL MEASUREMENT TECHNIQUES

A large number of potential indicators could be generated through the various permutations of the above strategies, though this will not be accomplished here. Instead, only one or two instances of each type of strategy will be explored. For example, while it is especially important in terms of welfare economics to adjust measures of income inequality for various factors of collective or subsidized income which are not accumulated in terms of money (e.g., health care, unemployment benefits, and social security-type programs), only the unadjusted measures will be generated below.[12]

2.41 *Gini Index*. Utilizing formula (2.1), two distinct Gini indices are constructed. Sector income inequality (GINISECT) was computed for

1970 from data on sector contribution to gross domestic product given (mostly) in the United Nations' *Yearbook of National Accounts Statistics* (1971). Sector work force data for 1970 or the nearest year were taken from the International Labour Organizations' *Handbook of Labour Statistics* (1972). Although some of the sector data were available only for years in the 1960s, they were utilized since they represent the best available data. Thus, 1970 should be looked at as a rough time slice rather than a firm cross-section. This problem no doubt introduces bias into the results. The Gini index for unadjusted, individual income (GININDIV) was computed from information given in Chenery et al. (1974). Therein, data is presented for sixty-six developing, market economies on the division of total income into the lower and middle forty percent and the top twenty percent of the population. This information, not the Gini, was used by Chenery to describe the distribution of wealth and poverty (separately) and their respective relationships to economic growth.

2.42 *Social Immobility Index.* This measure of social immobility (SOCIMOB) was taken directly from Gurr (forthcoming) as presented in Table 2.4.

2.43 *Hibbs' Z-Score Technique.* The calculation of this measure (HIBBZSCR) was nearly identical to the procedure suggested in Hibbs (1973) and adopted by Jackman (1975). There is one small refinement, however: infant mortality was used as a surrogate for live births *per* 1000.[13] Thus:

(**2.2**) HIBBZSCR = (INFMORT + DOCTORS + KILOCAL + PROTEIN)/D
where D = number of nonmissing observations for each case (D > 0),
and each variable is standardized.

2.44 *Ratios of Poverty and Affluence.* To operationalize the suggested ratio of poverty to affluence, two indicators need be constructed first.

    2.441 Aggregate Societal Affluence (AFFLU). From a host of variables measuring the extent of affluence in a country three were chosen: the number of Hilton Hotels, universities, and motor vehicle deaths (HILTON, UNVRSTY, and CARDTH, respectively). Each measure proposed reflects very high consumption levels—usually for the very

[31]

TABLE 2.4. *Social Immobility Index Values*[a]

SOCIAL IMMOBILITY SCORE	ADELMAN AND MORRIS CATEGORY	DEFINITION
0	none	School enrollment ratio (SER) 60%+ and middle class 30%+ and no substantial discrimination.
1	none	SER 60%+ or middle class 30%+, no discrimination.
2	none	SER 50–60% and middle class 20–30%, no discrimination.
3	A+	SER 50% or middle class 20–30%, no discrimination.
4	A	SER 40–50% and middle class 10–20%, no discrimination.
5	A–	Countries with A+ or A SER and middle class scores, but with marked discrimination.
6	none	High SER and middle class ratios, but with substantial discrimination.
7	B	SER 25–40%, middle class 5–10%, or countries meeting the first two criteria for A scores having discriminatory barriers to mobility.
8	none	Not used.
9	C+	SER greater than 25%, or very small but rapidly growing middle class.
10	C	SER less than 25% and very small middle class.
11	C–	SER less than 25%, small middle class, and extreme prohibitive barriers affecting the entire population.

a. Adapted from Gurr and Duvall (forthcoming).

rich within a nation. If there is a great deal of affluence, some of it will be reflected by absorptive markets such as leisure activity.

Needless to say, these are less than perfect indicators. For example, many countries that are not affluent have a strong tradition of higher learning; consequently, some fairly poor countries without any necessary distribution problems may have several important universities. The Middle Eastern countries (Islamic and non-Islamic alike) offer prime examples. However, these types of countries tend to have a few very old, large universities rather than an abundance of small universities such as are found in the United States. For this reason, the number of universities is potentially a better indicator than might appear at first glance.

The same type of argument might be lodged against the use of luxury hotels. But few countries have a great many nodes for foreign tourists—usually only one or two. If, however, one considers domestic tourists as indicative of leisure time activity, given that most countries will have at least a few for foreign tourists, the number of hotels should reflect certain facets of affluence within the polity. Motor vehicle deaths tend to be largely concentrated in accidents involving the use of automobiles for private rather than commercial transportation.

Table 2.5 presents the factor analysis of these three independent measures of societal affluence. The assertion that these three variables measure a similar type of attribute is born out by their intercorrelations. A single factor is extracted with which each of these variables is highly correlated. A composite index (AFFLU) was created by weighting the standardized variables by their factor loadings (a measure of their relative contribution to the factor covariance).[14] That is:

(2.3) $AFFLU = (.86(HILTON) + .86(UNVRSTY) + 1.003(CARDTH))/D$
where $D =$ number of non-missing observations
for each case, $(D > 0)$
and each variable is standardized.[15]

TABLE 2.5. *Principal Components Factor Analysis of Affluence Indicators**

AFFLUENCE VARIABLE	FACTOR LOADING
HILTON	86
UNVRSTY	86
CARDTH2	100
Pct of Total Var	91

*No rotation. Smallest n = 110.

All values except the eigenvalue are multiplied by 100.

All definitions are as previously defined. For extensive definition see Appendix B.

[33]

2.442 Aggregate Societal Poverty (POVRTY). A very nearly identical procedure has been employed in the analysis of this variable. Three variables were selected to reflect the extent of poverty in a social system. Those that were chosen relate to nutritional standards, since this represents one of the most basic of human needs. Kilocalories, grams of protein *per capita per diem*, and the average percentage of the minimum daily requirements adjusted for cultural and geographical factors were collected for 115 of the nations in the sample. The factor analysis of these variables is given in Table 2.6. This shows a very strong single factor solution—much like that for affluence.

2.443 Inequality Ratios (INEQ1 and INEQ2). The conceptual strategy for the mapping of the conjunction of affluence and poverty into inequality was presented above in Table 2.3. Having measured poverty and affluence it is necessary to choose the appropriate cutting points for each of the two variables. Failure to specify these values properly could potentially invalidate the entire approach. There is however no "correct" set of cutting points. In fact, the exact location of these points probably is determined by the specific cases under examination as much as by the purposes of the investigation. Herein, each variable was standardized (AFFLU and POVRTY), and those cases to the right of -1 standard deviations were scored low (1), between -1 and $+1$ were coded moderate (2), and the remainder were coded as high (3). The reason for choosing these particular

TABLE 2.6. *Principal Components Factor Analysis of Poverty Indicators**

POVERTY VARIABLE	FACTOR LOADING
KILOCAL	100
PROTEIN	81
REQPCT	93
Pct of Total Var	91

*No rotation. Smallest n = 110.

All values except the eigenvalue are multiplied by 100.

All variables are as previously defined. For extensive definitions see Appendix B.

cutting points is that a threefold classification was desired, since the conceptual map developed above (Table 2.3) contained three levels of aggregate societal poverty and affluence. From these scores and the conceptual map, the measure, INEQ1, was constructed.

By reference to Table 2.3 (above) this strategy becomes clearer. Each polity is assigned a score ranging from low to high on two variables, affluence and poverty. A score of 1 is low, 2 is medium, and 3 is high. Based upon a polity's score on both of these variables, an inequality score is assigned. Thus, a polity with low levels of poverty and low levels of affluence is assigned a low inequality score. The converse example, high poverty and high affluence, receives the highest possible inequality score (9).

Another measure of this ratio-type was created utilizing the ratio of telephones *per capita* (PHONETOT) for the entire polity to the number of telephones *per capita* in the major cities (PHONECITY). This index uses telephones as an indicator of economic, political, and social activity. If the telephones are concentrated in one major city, then by inference so are the bulk of these activities. This situation is one which is characteristic of inequality.[16] The index, INEQ2, is given by:

(2.4)   INEQ2 = PHONETOT − PHONECITY.

Having constructed these independent measures of inequality, the task at hand is to explore their interrelationships. This will be accomplished in the next section.

2.5 EMPIRICAL EVALUATION OF MEASUREMENT TECHNIQUES

This section offers several formal hypotheses about the indicators developed above. These hypotheses are evaluated in a similar fashion to what has been termed the "Campbell-Fiske" methodology (1959). However, their proposed strategy is not entirely appropriate here inasmuch as only one type of phenomenon is being examined by a host of methods rather than several phenomena by several methods.[17] The ultimate goal is the evaluation of the clustering of the above indicators from an empirical perspective in order to assess their unidimensionality. This should provide useful information about the validity and reliability of the measurement.

[35]

The first set of hypotheses to be examined is concerned with the validity of the poverty and affluence indicators. The logic of the final construction of the inequality ratio, INEQ1, was based in part on the discovery/creation of valid and reliable indicators of these two concepts. Thus:

H1 : Multiple indicators of affluence are strongly positively associated.

H2 : Multiple indicators of poverty are strongly positively associated.

Furthermore, the conceptual argument asserts that poverty and affluence are independent attributes of social units which are present in various degrees in all societies. However, they are somewhat covariant, since a great deal of affluence is often accompanied by a great deal of poverty. Yet, all combinations of these two variables are theoretically possible—and in fact almost all are observable in the referent data set. Thus, one would expect a weak to moderate positive association between affluence and poverty. Formally,

H3 : Indicators of poverty will be weakly, positively associated with indicators of affluence.

Given the Campbell-Fiske orientation, one would also expect that:

H4 : Intercorrelations among similar traits will be greater than across traits.

Table 2.7 presents the intercorrelations among the poverty and affluence variables. Factor analyses presented in Tables 2.5 and 2.6 also give a certain amount of confirmation to H1 and H2, representing as they do single factor solutions. Table 2.7 further corroborates this in addition to demonstrating the strength of H4.

Both H1 and H2 are strongly supported by this evidence. For each concept, poverty and affluence, the lowest intra-indicator correlation is a robust 0.72. Hypothesis 3 is also supported, since all the cross-concept correlations are less than 0.44. However, there does seem to be moderate correlation between UNVRSTY and all of the poverty indicators. The other two affluence indicators are statistically more independent, with the highest cross concept coefficient being 0.3. This does support H3 inasmuch as it was predicted that some positive covariation would exist, but that if it were substantial, either the data,

TABLE 2.7. *Intercorrelations of Affluence and Poverty Indicators for 120 Contemporary Polities (1970)* *

Poverty Indicators:						
KILOCAL		110	110	110	109	59
PROTEIN	82		110	110	109	59
REQPCT	95	72		110	109	59
Affluence Indicators:						
HILTON	19	20	17		118	64
UNVRSTY	43	44	40	72		62
CARDTH2	29	30	29	88	88	

*Ns are given above the diagonal; Pearson product-moment correlation coefficients (multiplied by 100) below.

All variables are as previously defined. For extensive definitions, see Appendix B.

instrument, or conceptual strategy would be suspect. The fourth hypothesis is also strongly supported by Table 2.7. All inter-indicator correlations are greater than any cross-concept correlations. The mean poverty inter-indicator correlation is 0.86, the mean correlation for affluence indicators is 0.83, while the average cross-concept is 0.3. Thus, individually as well as on an average, H3 is strongly supported. Not only the rationale of the construction of INEQ1, but its empirics as well seem borne out.

Apart from empirical examination of any single indicator of inequality, it is important to examine the entire set of indices that were advanced from the conceptual analysis. In general, they should each be strongly and positively associated. One should not however expect the scores to be identical, or even nearly so, inasmuch as it has been shown that sector income underestimates actual inequality by assuming perfect equality within any one sector.

H5 : Empirical indicators of inequality should covary in a positive fashion.

To examine this hypothesis, H5, the Pearson product-moment correlations were generated and are presented in Table 2.8. The intercorrelations in Table 2.8 show a very strong degree of association, with the exception of the measure of sector inequality (GINISECT). This is most notable since this examination presents the first empirical evi-

TABLE 2.8. *Intercorrelations of Inequality Indicators**

	INEQ2	SOCIMOB	HIBBZSCR	INEQ1	GININDIV	GINISECT
INEQ2		77	76	98	56	77
SOCIMOB	58		73	85	56	75
HIBBZSCR	66	70		89	56	75
INEQ1	55	62	85		64	91
GININDIV	37	43	62	51		58
GINISECT	08	07	10	-13	01	

Ns are given above the diagonal; Pearson product-moment correlation coefficients (multiplied by 100) are given below the diagonal.

*Each of these indices is designed to reflect the extent of inequality in the distribution of valued goods within contemporary polities:

  INEQ2 is a measure of inequality of telephone service obtained by dividing the average number of telephones per 100 inhabitants in 1970 by the average number of telephones per 100 inhabitants in the capital city of the relevant polity;
  SOCIMOB is a measure of the extent of social immobility within a polity as explicitly defined in Table 2.4;
  HIBBZSCR is an adaptation of a measure suggested by D. Hibbs (1973) which utilizes infant mortality, the number of doctors per 10,000 inhabitants, the number of kilocalories per head per day, and the percent of daily requirements per head;
  INEQ1 is an inequality index defined by a ration of poverty to affluence, as explicitly defined in Table 2.3;
  GININDIV is a Gini index of income inequality based upon the family income shares held by the top 20, middle 40, and lower 40 percent of the population;
  GINISECT is a sector-based Gini index of income inequality utilizing 1970 data on two subcomponents, the size of the work force in each sector and the gross domestic product generated in each sector.

All variables are as previously defined. For extensive definitions see Appendix B.

dence (and test) of Kuznets' original assertions about inferring wealth inequality from sector product. In particular, we should find sector and individual income inequality to be strongly associated. Instead, we observe that they do not appear to be related in any fashion. This hypothesis, H5, must be rejected. The Kuznets-based indicator is not correlated strongly with any of the other indicators of inequality. This might not seem critical if there were little or no variation among the other indicators. However, this is not the case. It seems clear that GINISECT shares virtually no covariation with other measures of inequality. Figure 2.3 presents the scatterplot, regression line, and 95 percent confidence intervals of the sector and individual income inequality measures, GINISECT and GININDIV. This visually reinforces the interpretation of random covariance. In fairness, it must be remembered that Kuznets (1963) as well as Taylor and Hudson (1972) have warned about inferring individual income inequalities from these

FIGURE 2.2. Scatterplot of Individual (GININDIV) and
Sectoral (GINISECT) Gini Scores

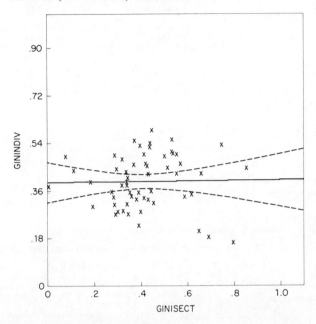

sector-based data. This finding does present firm evidence that one
may not correctly do so—rather than arguing that it may be an incorrect inference. This finding may be viewed as somewhat startling,
given the strong implications it holds for empirical studies that have
used sector income as an approximation to individual income.

Deleting GINISECT from the set of potential inequality indicators as
being empirically unsound, the remaining set shows strong covariation. The mean intercorrelation of the reduced set is 0.55. The scatterplots of each two indicators in the reduced set were examined for
any extreme cases which could grossly affect these conclusions. The
only exception was the United States, which has a disproportionately
high number of telephones in a few major cities—in particular,
Washington and New York. The unidimensionality of this reduced set
of indicators is shown by the factor analysis presented in Table 2.9.
This single factor solution is remarkably similar to the previous
ones—a strong single factor emerges.[18]

One further problem that might bias the results is the pooling of the
market and nonmarket economies. Most economists and many politi-

TABLE 2.9. *Principal Components Analysis of Inequality Indicators**

VARIABLE	FACTOR	COMMUNALITY
INEQ2	68	46
SOCIMOB	75	56
HIBB2SCR	98	96
INEQ1	85	72
GININDIV	60	36
Pct of Total Var	77	

*No rotation. Smallest n = 53.

All values except the eigenvalue are multiplied by 100.

All variables are as previously defined. For extensive definitions see Appendix B.

cal scientists refuse to combine these two polities in their analyses. The reasons for this are somewhat complex since "price" and "value" have different absolute meanings in the two types of economies.[19] Also, aside from the comparability of the data, it is difficult to obtain much of the nonmarket data. This is a somewhat self-fulfilling prophecy, since economists and many political scientists do not collect or collate it.

The position taken here is that, in principle, it is possible to measure economic types of variables for both types of economic systems. The comparability may not be perfect, yet it will offer some evidence about both types of economies. The distinction between market and nonmarket is in fact not a simple one, since most economic systems in the late 1960s and early 1970s tend to combine many facets of both styles. Since the role of governmental policy making should (*viz.,* Jackman (1975)) have a lot to do with the distribution of valued objects/outcomes/goods, one ought not to exclude a certain class of cases from the study on *a priori* grounds that they are not comparable. Even further, when a cross section is being used to approximate a causal process, this exclusion has extremely severe implications. Moreover, the multiplicity of measurement attacks presented here is not dominated by financial statistics. Consequently, all types of countries have been included in the analysis.

The correlation matrix of the indicators of inequality for market economies was examined. The results, presented in Table 2.10, show that the entire sample and the market economies separately are virtually identical with respect to this index. However, one interesting difference is that the correlation between the two Gini measures shows a substantial increase in size when the nonmarket economies are deleted (0.01 vs 0.30). This suggests that the sector income and individual income are much more closely related in market economies. Kuznets' original work, it must be remembered, dealt only with market economies. His original assertion is, then, supported weakly.

Jackman notes a similar point when discussing a shortcoming in his book:

> [The] decision over which countries to include leads to the *de facto* exclusion of all countries with communist regimes. While some data are available on income equality for such countries, Kuznets has argued that comparisons of these data across communist and noncommunist regimes is not altogether meaningful because data are collected according to different criteria within the two categories. This then leads to an important restriction on the study, in that we are unable to examine one set of propositions about the poitical determinants of social equality that involves a major twentieth-century series of political movements which have been publicly and explicitly concerned with precisely the issue of the redistribution of material rewards itself [1975:10]

It is hoped that this study will not face the same severe limitations, since both communist and noncommunist regimes are included in this analysis, which itself shows consistent results across these two sets of polities.

TABLE 2.10. *Intercorrelations Among Inequality Indicators for Market Economies*

INEQ2		71	70	92	52	71
SOCIMOB	57		66	78	52	68
HIBB2SCR	64	70		82	49	68
INEQ1	52	61	82		60	84
GININDIV	35	43	50	38		54
GINISECT	19	18	12	04	30	

Ns are given above the diagonal; Pearson product-moment correlations (multiplied by 100) below.

All variables are as previously defined. For extensive definitions, see Appendix B.

[41]

One plausible probe of the utility of the aforementioned assumption about the possibility of measuring nonmarket economies is to perform an analysis of variance using the market-nonmarket division as a grouping technique. However, even if the index were completely free of comparability problems across these two types of economic arrangements, there would be no *a priori* reason to expect any particular patterns of covariance. That is, it seems likely that there might be theoretical as opposed to artificial reasons why communist nations as a group may potentially score differently than the Western market economies on this index. The assumption that these two types of economic systems may be compared, then, cannot be examined in a purely methodological vein. This assumption can only be examined in a theory laden analysis. Accordingly, more attention will be given to this question in subsequent chapters. Moreover, once the indicator of societal inequality to be used in this study is constructed, it will be easier to examine the potential market-nonmarket bias of the index.

Ultimately, however, since this assertion is not testable without considerable theoretical specification of what differences, if any, might be reasonably expected to exist, it seems important to stress that the objections of many to comparing market with nonmarket economies is based upon the differences across these systems which exist between financial accounting techniques as well as between the more fundamental social meaning of value. The latter is a thorny issue unlikely to be easily resolved. The former, however, should not plague this study, since little reliance is placed upon accounting techniques by this indexing procedure.

All of the analyses above suggest that the reduced set of indicators share a great deal of common variance. Based upon this examination, a weighted composite indicator of inequality (INEQUAL) was computed in which the weights are derived from the factor loadings presented in Table 2.9:[20]

(2.5)   INEQUAL = (0.68(INEQ2) +
0.75(SOCIMOB) +
0.98(HIBBZSCR) +
0.85(INEQ1) +
0.60(GININDIV))/D
where D = number of nonmissing observations for each case (D > 0), and each variable is standardized.

TABLE 2.11. *Inequality Index (INEQUAL) for 120 Polities, by Level of Gross National Product Per Capita**

COUNTRY IDENTIFIER AND INEQUALITY SCORE
1970 Gross National Product *Per Capita*

GREATER THAN $1,200		BETWEEN $1,200 AND $300		LESS THAN $300			
USA	−138	ROM	−88	IVO	32	ETH	35
SWE	−69	VEN	24	DOM	49	NIG	−12
CAN	−95	BUL	−94	ZAM	44	IND	44
ICE	−6	GRC	−84	GHA	55	NGA	48
SWI	−165	SPA	−34	KON	29	TAN	57
LUX	−106	SAF	21	KOS	8	BUR	48
FRN	−95	LEB	19	ALG	101	BOT	15
DEN	−85	CHI	4	PHI	40	VOL	120
NOR	−62	URU	−11	TUN	26	SIN	−1
GMW	−74	ANG	−88	BOL	110	ZAI	95
AUL	−93	CUB	−11	MRC	58	MLW	53
IRE	7	MEX	23	ZIM	48	BRD	27
BEL	−108	COS	8	EGY	30	CAR	64
NET	−85	SAU	29	CAO	74	CEY	24
UNK	−97	YUG	−72	TAI	31	CHA	43
CZE	−117	PAN	40	VTS	76	CON	42
USR	−102	POR	−34	SYR	35	CYP	55
FIN	−87	JAM	29	ECU	98	DAH	40
GME	−101	NIC	41	CAM	63	GAB	63
PUE	−27	HOK	25	MGY	51	GAM	50
ISR	−88	ALB	11	SUD	63	LAO	47
NEW	−81	JOR	42	AFG	120	LES	−8
AUS	−108	PAR	32	PAK	44	LIB	122
JAP	−50	TUR	−31	CHN	29	SIE	55
ITA	−122	HON	63	LBY	37	SOM	89
HUN	−102	GUA	70	UGA	33	YES	89
POL	−96	BHO	46	YEN	93		
		MLY	29	VTN	29		
		PER	49	KEN	58		
		BRA	22	INS	93		
		CHT	−15				

[43]

TABLE 2.11. *Inequality Index (INEQUAL) for 120 Polities, by Level of Gross National Product Per Capita* (cont.)*

COUNTRY IDENTIFIER AND INEQUALITY SCORE
1970 Gross National Product *Per Capita*

GREATER THAN $1,200	BETWEEN $1,200 AND $300		LESS THAN $300
	IRQ	62	
	IRN	34	
	COL	36	
	ELS	69	
	SEN	55	
	GUI	123	

*Scores have been multiplied by 100 to eliminate the decimal.

The new index is highly correlated (greater than 0.7) with each of its components.

Table 2.11 presents the scores on this new inequality index, grouped by the level of 1970 GNP *per capita* for each of the 120 polities that comprise this study. One prominent feature of inequality in these contemporary nations, as measured by this index, is the low levels of inequality exhibited by nations with average productivity of greater than $1,200. Ranging from the U.S.A. to Poland, virtually all of these nations have low levels of inequality, though there is marked variation in the exact scores. The polities with GNP figures in the $1,299 to $300 range tend to have greater levels of inequality. The largest category, nations with less than $200 GNP *per capita*, tend to have very high levels of inequality.

While these three groupings tend to be suggestive of a strong link between inequality and the average level of national productivity, each group shows marked variability.

Table 2.12 presents a breakdown of inequality by geographical region. These data show a world of great diversity in the inequality within nations. One of the most interesting characteristics that the sample exhibits is the clustering of European nations, all of which have low levels of inequality—irrespective of economic organization. More specifically, European market economies have a mean inequality score

TABLE 2.12. *Inequality by Geographic Region and Market Organization*

REGION	MEAN	STANDARD DEVIATION
Latin America (n=22)	.34	.35
Asia (n=20)	.36	.37
Middle East and North Africa (n=13)	.51	.27
Africa (n=20)	.72	.40
European market economies (n=27)	−.72	.49
European centrally planned economies (n=8)	−.86	.40
ETA^2 = .66		
F = 44.47 (p<.0000)		

of −.72 as compared to a score of −.86 for the nonmarket communist polities in Europe. Not only are the means in the same range, but the in-group variances are roughly equal as well (respectively .12 and .16). Thus, it would appear that compared to the entire range of inequality, the level of inequality in market economies is roughly identical to that in nonmarket economies.

In summary, inequality itself is distributed in an unequal though patterned fashion. The European polities consistently have less inequality than other polities. Roughly, the often hypothesized relationship between development and equality seems to be reinforced by this evidence. This will be formally explored in much greater detail in the following chapters.

NOTES

1. Hollis Chenery and his associates (1974,1975) have produced a compendium of recent work. See particularly, *Redistribution with Growth*, Oxford University Press.
2. It should be pointed out that Duvall explores the meaning of each term is his definition: social, realization, goods, and entities.
3. See the works of Mitchell (1968); Paige (1970); Russo (1972); Paranzino (1972); and finally (?) Nagel (1974).
4. The tension here is between those who would argue that one's analytics and empirics

ought not interact at all levels of inquiry, including the measurement level and those who argue that the chain from analytics to measurement to observation and back again has no necessary, one-step feedback. That is, measurement ought not to influence one's analytics nor should actual measurements (observations) affect one's measurement instruments (techniques). Thus, the Gini is often both attractive and unattractive to different sets of scholars for this single reason: it is little influenced by our perceptions of the "realities" of inequality.

5. To demonstrate, consider a two actor system wherein the poorest social unit comprises 70 percent of the total population and possesses 30 percent of the total wealth. The area below the Lorenz curve is represented by the following:

   Area = $2(2Y - X - Y + 1)$ where $Y = 30$ and $X = 70$.

   For the given condition, this yields an area of 0.3 and a Gini score of 0.4. If this area is 0.3, one can choose any X and solve for the Y value which will describe the Lorenz curve, and has an identical Gini score. Thus, select an X equal to 0.8, the resultant Y = 0.4, and the calculated Gini score is 0.4. The severity of this instability does however diminish as the number of actors increases. It does not disappear entirely.

6. These data were provided by Inousha Chintakananda through personal communication.

7. See Jackman (1975:14ff) for a discussion of this index.

8. Although unlike the Schutz coefficient, the smallest proportion of the population with half of the wealth (i.e., the miminal majority) is not analytically equivalent to the Gini index, it is empirically equivalent. Alker and Russett (1967) report a correlation of 0.95 between the two. Thus, it is essentially redundant. Further, since typically researchers are dealing with sectoral data (i.e., n = 8 or less), the minimal majority index represents a large conceptual leap—although technically one could establish fiducial intervals bounding its values. They would be too large to prove useful.

9. Gurr (1968:1110) first discussed and utilized this type of technique in exploring the determinants of civil strife; Janda (1971) has explored some of its statistical implications; and Levine (1973) has further discussed the statistical utility of such an approach.

10. See Taylor and Hudson (1972:214).

11. The assumptions in this assignment rule are relatively clear. Many researchers who find that these assumptions are totally (or partially) unfounded will no doubt challenge them. The flexibility which is built into this strategy does allow the modification of the indexing rule to fit individual needs.

12. For example, Nelson et al. note:
   Personal income includes income from property and entrepreneurial services as well as wages and salaries. It would be highly desirable to have separate data on the distribution of such income, but unfortunately these are not available for Colombia. The problem of obtaining reliable information on the distribution of property and entrepreneurial income is not, of course, specific to Colombia. Income distribution data from surveys and censuses tend, in general, to miss a greater fraction of property and entreprenerial income than wage income. Although this component is not much more than a quarter of total personal income, it forms a significant portion of the highest income recipients. Thus income distribution surveys tend to have a downward bias to their estimates of the income share of the upper income brackets. This bias is aggravated when, as often happens, the survey was designed originally to report on labor force characteristics or consumption patterns rather than the distribution of income [1971:140].

13. This measure has been rescaled to reflect inequality rather than equality.

14. It is recognized that the communalities should be used as weights since they repre-

sent the precise amount of shared variance between each variable and the underlying factor. However, it was found that this statistical "refinement" was unnecessary in one sense, because it produced equivalent results. More precisely, an index of affluence was constructed using as weights the communalities rather than the loadings. The two indices were correlated greater than 0.97. Rather than implying that these two procedures are analytically equivalent, this result only demonstrates their empirical overlap with respect to this particular cluster of variables in this specific data set. As such, the overlap is representative in great part of the strength and unidimensionality of the underlying dimension, i.e., aggregate societal affluence.

Since what follows in terms of index construction is logically and serially ordered, one further observation will be made at this point concerning this problem. For each subsequent factor analysis presented in this chapter, both techniques were examined. In no instance was the correlation between techniques less than 0.96. Further, one later analysis involves the construction of an index which is itself in part based upon earlier indices constructed through this procedure. In that case, the two solutions, i.e., factor loadings *versus* communalities as weights at each successive stage, were correlated 0.99. It must be stressed again that this is an empirical finding which is analytically linked to the coherence and strength of an underlying factor structure which is unidimensional.

15. Since the communalities exceed 1.0 for this factor, the factor score itself is basically meaningless. The mean Z-score technique was modified to construct this index. The modified technique provides additional information because the weights of the components are not assumed to be equal (i.e., 1.0); rather, they are empirically derived.

16. A similar measure was originally suggested to me by Farid Abolfathi.

17. These difficulties have been spoken to in Althauser, Heberlein, and Scott (1971), and Ward (1974).

18. All of the factor analyses in this chapter are based upon correlation matrices generated through a pairwise deletion procedure. This procedure can significantly bias the results. The listwise correlation matrix (no missing data) was examined to test the importance of this bias:

INEQ2

SOCIMOB	63				
HIBBZSCR	62	68			
INEQ1	43	54	85		
GINISECT	29	41	58	48	
GININDIV	07	20	02	−10	04

This matrix shows the same basic pattern as presented in Table 2.7. Accordingly, the factor solution (not presented here) is virtually identical to the one presented above.

19. See Pryor (1968, 1971) for an explanation as well as some empirical work on economic data from communist countries.

20. The procedure employed here is identical to that described above for the weighted factor scores on poverty and affluence. One further observation bears mention. There is one fairly deviant case for INEQ2: as mentioned before, the United States has an extreme value on this index. Although it might be omitted on grounds that it unduly influences the final index, no cases with "extreme" values were excluded from the composite index. The rationale for this is that since a multiple indicator is used to modulate the influence of indicators of varying potence for particular cases it would be self-defeating to discard "extreme" cases. Further, one might argue that it would be superfluous.

[47]

REFERENCES

Adelman, I. and C. Morris (1973). Economic Growth and Social Equity in Developing Countries. Stanford, California: Stanford University Press.

Akins, J.E. (1973). "The Oil Crises: This Time the Wolf is Here." Foreign Affairs, Vol. 51, No. 3, pp 462-490.

Alker, H.R., (1965). Mathematics and Politics. New York: Macmillan.

Alker, H.R. and B.M. Russett (1966). "Indices for Comparing Inequality," in Richard Merritt and Stein Rokkan (eds.), Comparing Nations. New Haven, Conn.: Yale University Press.

Althauser, R., T. Heberlein, and R. Scott (1971). "A Causal Assessment of Validity: The Augmented Multitrait-Multimethod Matrix," in Hubert M. Blalock (ed.), Causal Models in the Social Sciences. Chicago, Illinois: Aldine Publishers.

Barber, B. (1975). "Justifying Justice: Problems of Psychology, Measurement, and Politics in Rawls." American Political Science Review, Vol. 69, No. 2, pp 663-674.

Boudon, R. (1974). Education, Opportunities, and Social Inequality: Changing Prospects in Western Society, a translation of L'inegalite des Chances, by the author. New York: John Wiley.

Campbell, D.T. and D.W. Fiske (1959). "Convergent and Discriminant Validation by the Multitrait-Multimethod Matrix," reprinted in G. Summers (ed.), Attitude Measurement. Chicago, Illinois: Rand McNally.

Chenery, H., M.S. Ahluwalia, C.L.G. Bell, J.H. Duloy, and R. Jolly (1974). Redistribution with Growth. New York: Oxford University Press.

Chenery, H., M. Syrquin with H. Elkington (1975). Patterns of Development, 1950-1970. New York: Oxford University Press.

Chintakananda, Inoushu (1976). Unpublished Ph.D. dissertation, Northwestern University.

Chiswick, B.R. (1974). Income Inequality: Regional Analysis within a Human Capital Framework, NBER. New York: Columbia University Press.

Cook, K.S. (1975). "Expectations, Evaluations, and Equity." American Sociological Review, Vol. 40, pp 372-388.

Cutright, P. (1967). "Inequality: A Cross-National Analysis." American Sociological Review, Vol. 32, pp 562-578.

Drewnowski, J. and W. Scott (1966). The Level of Living Index. Geneva: UNISD Report 4.

Duvall, R. (1975). International Stratification: Concept and Theory. Unpublished Ph.D. dissertation, Northwestern University.

Elliot, C. (1975). Patterns of Poverty in the Third World. New York: Praeger Publishers.

Emmanuel, A. (1972). Unequal Exchange: A Study of the Imperialism of Trade. New York: Monthly Review Press.

Galtung, J (1971). "A Structural Theory of Imperialism." Journal of Peace Research, Vol. 7, No. 2, pp 81-117.

Galtung, J., A. Guha, A. Wirak, S. Sjlie, M. Cifuentes, and H. Goldstein (1975). "Measuring World Development - Part I and II." Alternatives, Vol. 1, Nos. 1 and 4, pp 131-158, 523-555.

Gini, C. (1936). "On the Measurement of Concentration with Especial Reference to Income and Wealth."

Gurr, T.R. (1966). New Error-Compensated Measures for Comparing Nations: Some

Correlates of Civil Violence. Princeton, New Jersey: Princeton University Press, Center of International Studies Research Monograph 25.

Gurr, T.R. (1968). "A Causal Model of Civil Strife: A Comparative Analysis Using New Indices." American Political Science Review, Vol. 62, pp 1104-1124.

Gurr, T.R. (1970). Why Men Rebel. Princeton, New Jersey: Princeton University Press.

Gurr, T.R. and R. Duvall (1973). "Civil Conflict in the 1960s: A Complete Theoretical System with Parameter Estimates." Comparative Political Studies, Vol. 6, No. 2, pp 135-169.

Gurr, T.R. and R. Duvall (forthcoming). Nations in Conflict.

Hibbs, D.A. (1973). Mass Political Violence. New York: John Wiley.

Hoivik, Tord (1971). "Social Inequality: The Main Issues." Journal of Peace Research, Vol. 7, No. 2, pp 119-142.

Horowitz, I. (1971). "On Numbers-Equivalents and the Concentration Ratio: An International Empirical Comparison." Quarterly Review of Economics and Business, Vol. 10, No. 3, pp 55-63.

International Labour Office (1974). Yearbook of Labour Statistics. Geneva:ILO.

International Labour Office (1977). Employment, Growth, and Basic Needs: A One-World Problem. New York: Praeger for the Overseas Development Council in cooperation with the International Labour Office.

Jackman, R.W. (1975). Politics and Social Equality. New York: John Wiley.

Janda, K. (1971). "A Technique for Assessing the Conceptual Equivalence of Institutional Variables across and within Culture Areas." Paper prepared for delivery at the 1971 Annual Meetings of the American Political Science Association, Chicago, Illinois, September 7-11.

Jencks, Christopher, et al. (1972). Inequality: A Reassessment of the Effect of Family and Schooling in America. New York: Basic Books.

Kuhn, T. (1962). The Structure of Scientific Revolutions. Chicago, Illinois: University of Chicago Press, Phoenix edition.

Kuznets, S. (1963). "Quantitative Aspects of the Economic Growth of Nations, VIII: The Distribution of Income by Size." Economic Development and Cultural Change, Vol. 11, part 2 (entire).

Levine, M.S. (1973). "Standard Scores as Indices: The Pitfalls of Not Thinking it Through." American Journal of Political Science, Vol. 17, No. 2.

Mitchell, E.J. (1968). "Inequality and Insurgency, A Statistical Study of South Vietnam." World Politics, Vol. 20, pp 421-438.

Morgan, W. and J. Sawyer (1967). "Bargaining, Expectation, and the Preference for Equality over Equity." Journal of Personal and Social Psychology, pp 139-149.

Nagel, J. (1974). "Inequality and Discontent: A Nonlinear Hypothesis." World Politics, Vol. 26, No. 4, pp 453-472.

Nordhaus, W. and J. Tobin (1972). "Is Growth Obsolete?" in Economic Growth, Fiftieth Anniversary Colloquium V, NBER. New York: Columbia University Press.

Nelson, R.T., T.P. Schultz, and R. Slighton (1971). Structural Change in a Developing Economy. Princeton, New Jersey: Princeton University Press.

Paige, J.M. (1970). "Inequality and Insurgency in Vietnam: A Reanalysis." World Politics, Vol. 23, No. 1, pp 24-37.

Paranzino, D. (1972). "Inequality and Insurgency in Vietnam: A Further Reanalysis." World Politics, Vol. 24, pp 565-578.

Pennock, J.R. (1966). "Political Development, Political Systems, and Political Goods." World Politics, Vol. 18, pp 415-434.

Pryor, F.L. (1968). Public Expenditures in Communist and Capitalist Nations. Homewood, Illinois: Richard D. Irwin. Vol. 69, No. 2, pp 630-648.

Pryor, F.L. (1971). "Economic System and the Size Distribution of Income and Wealth." Bloomington, Indiana: International Development Research Center, Working Paper Series.

Rawls, J. (1971). A Theory of Justice. Cambridge, Mass.: Harvard University Press.

Russett, B.M. (1964). "Inequality and Instability: The Relation of Land Tenure to Politics." World Politics, Vol. 16, No. 3, pp 442-454.

Russo, A.J. (1972). "Economic and Social Correlates of Governmental Control in South Vietnam," in I.K. Feierabend, R.L. Feierabend, and T.R. Gurr (eds.), Anger, Violence, and Politics, Englewood Cliffs, N.J.: Prentice-Hall, 1972, pp 314-324.

Schiller, B.R. (1970). "Stratified Opportunities- The Essence of the 'Vicious Circle'." American Journal of Sociology, Vol. 76, No. 3, pp 426-442.

Taussig, M.K. (1973). Alternative Measures of the Distribution of Economic Welfare. Industrial Relations Section, Princeton University Research Report Series No. 116.

Taylor, C.L. and M.C. Hudson (1972). World Handbook of Political and Social Indicators, 2nd edition. New Haven, Conn.: Yale University Press.

Tinbergen, J. (1976). RIO: Reshaping the International Order: A Report to the Club of Rome. New York: E.P. Dutton.

Tonelson, A. (1977). "Who Needs Basic Needs?" The Interdependent, Vol. 5, No. 1:1ff.

United Nations (1970). Yearbook of National Accounts Statistics. Vol. III: International Tables, New York: United Nations.

Ward, Michael (1974). "Authority Dimensions: A Study of the Reliability and Validity of the Polity Data." Northwestern University, mimeo.

Woodhouse, E.J. (1972). "Re-visioning the Future of the Third World: An Ecological Perspective on Development." World Politics, Vol. 25, No. 1, pp 1-34.

Societal Inequality within Contemporary Nations: Economic Development and Its Impact

3

3.1 INTRODUCTION

This chapter explores the aggregate relationship between the economic development of a nation and the extent to which economic and social goods are equally distributed within it.[1] One prominent line of argument starts with the assumption that unless there is a considerable amount of economic product which is generated within a society, there is very little point in talking about that society's distributive capacity. Further, in societies at "early" stages of development the distributive function tends to be highly inegalitarian. Among the several reasons offered for this assertion three stand out: (1) underdeveloped economic structures tend to be politically undifferentiated and consequently demonstrate little effective political mobilization through such mechanisms as trade unions or mass political parties which could potentially make demands for a wider dispersion of the economic and social product; (2) underdevelopment tends to be bureaucratic as well as economic and political. Thus, often the governmental structure which could be used as a policy tool to expand the dispersion of the economic and social product is either inadequate or totally absent; and (3) the wealthier members of society tend to accumulate marginal product at a much higher rate than do the impoverished. The poor must utilize virtually all of their income for maintenance, while the wealthy require only a small portion of their income for day-to-day expenses such as food, clothing, and shelter, and therefore can save the rather large portion of their income. Not only do the poor find it more difficult to save, but also there is little opportunity for them to make money through investments requiring sizable commitments of capital.

The process of development is said to accelerate this tendency for inegalitarian distributions of social goods by rewarding the already wealthy segments for their investments in a growing economic structure. Also, urbanization and industrialization center much of the new labor and wealth on a few locations, while the rest of society is either neglected or retarded. Finally, as the economic growth begins to level off and the desired goal of "development" is approached, the bureaucratic and political development begins to "catch up" with the economic growth. Since this occurrence comes at a time in which presumably there is a stable and diversified economic structure, whatever new demands are made by nascent interest groups are much more likely to be met by the established bureaucracy since it not only is equipped with expertise, but also possesses an expanding resource base aimed at enhancing its ability to make changes in the distributive process which might lead to a greater level of equality. The argument that there is diminishing equality at early stages of development is based largely upon the notion that preindustrial societies were highly egalitarian in the sense that virtually everybody tilled for themselves that which they consumed. Such accounts have been largely dismissed by political economists as inaccurate renditions of preindustrial economies. For the most part the treatment of this curvilinear hypothesis in the literature has dealt with the extent to which equality was enhanced by increasing levels of postindustrial development. While there are variants to this argument, in general it characterizes what is often known as the curvilinear hypothesis which relates development to equality.

This assessment of the relationship between development and inequality is optimistic on the one hand and naive on the other. There are many important influences other than economic development that impinge upon the distribution process. Most notable among these are two sets of constraints: (1) internal structural political constraints, such as the bureaucratic and governmental structures as well as the social philosophy of the decision-making elite, and (2) international impingements upon the scope and effectiveness of internal policy making such as alliance structures and trade patterns.

[52]

Even with these recognized shortcomings, the basic curvilinear relationship relating development and inequality is a valuable starting point for the investigation of the domestic and international causes of inequality within national political units. The choice of this particular starting point is important for several reasons. First, it has been the cornerstone of much of the extant empirical and theoretical work on inequality (*viz*. Kuznets, 1955, 1963; Adelman and Morris, 1967, 1973; Jackman, 1975). Thus, there is a foundation upon which to build future explorations. Second, it is the development process itself, as embodied in the economic successes of the Western, industrial powers, that has provided a goal—perhaps undesirable—which elites of underdeveloped nation-states have, for the most part though not singularly, attempted to emulate in order to achieve growth in the level of prosperity and, when coupled with their political ideologies, equality. Finally, development has been one of the major facets of North-South interaction. Accordingly, it structures many of the interactions and transactions of both the developing and the developed worlds. For these reasons then, this chapter will explore the relationship between development and societal inequality by building upon and extending previous work. Three basic areas will be explored in order to cumulatively build and test a model relating economic development and societal inequality: (1) the level of development; (2) short-term fluctuation in domestic economic activity; and (3) the diversification of the economic structure.

3.2 THE IMPACT OF THE LEVEL OF DEVELOPMENT

Simon Kuznets (1955, 1963) was among the first modern social scientists to explore the relationship between the distribution of wealth and the process of socioeconomic development. In fact, few subsequent analyses have failed to acknowledge their debt to his pioneering scholarship. This research also begins with the ideas of Simon Kuznets as a cornerstone.

Two primary facets motivate the general statement made by Kuznets. First, the argument posits that wealthier segments of the population tend to accumulate or save a greater proportion of any increased productivity which is due to economic development. This argument has been reiterated almost to the point of canonization in the "principle" that the rich tend to save and the poor tend to spend whatever marginal product they each might accrue. The second underpinning is that since development often leads not only to increased industrialization but also to increased levels of urbanization, there is a concomitant "urbanization" of wealth. That is, urban centers increasingly become the most productive sectors of the economy, thereby causing a migration of a substantial portion of the work force out of the poorer, rural areas that are largely agricultural and into the richer, industrialized ones. This argument provides the nexus of the often invoked "dual economy" theory. On the basis of these two theoretically informed hypotheses, Kuznets, and Myrdal (1953, 1973) as well, argue that there is increasing inequality effected at early (preindustrial) stages of growth which may be largely explained by the concentration of that growth into the industrial, urban areas. Only during the more advanced, industrial stages of growth is there any increase in equality of income brought about by increased economic development.

Based upon admittedly sparse empirical evidence and much conjecture, Kuznets concluded that there had been a narrowing of inequality which accompanied the process of development:

> In the absence of evidence to the contrary, I assume that it is true: that the secular income structure is somewhat more unequal in underdeveloped countries than in the more advanced—particularly in those of Western and Northern Europe and their economically developed descendants in the New World (the United States, Canada, Australia and New Zealand) [1955:23].

This conclusion does not easily follow from the two previous hypotheses about the structure of a dual economy. In fact, the dual economy hypothesis suggests, other things being equal, that as a country initially develops, there will be increasing concentration of wealth within the urban, industrial sector, and hence increasing inequality. The empirical evidence, such as it was, suggested that the opposite was true: development seemed to increase the equality of wealth.

It is at this point that many scholars part company with the theory of Kuznets, yet Kuznets argues that his empirically based conclusion was consistent with the dual economy model as he portrayed it. The basic contradiction is resolved by careful examination of the influences contributing to the declining relative share of wealth held by those in the social structure who are already wealthy. Three basic characteristics of a growing, dynamic, and, thereby, developing economy are

[54]

discussed. Population growth is necessary to increase the labor pool. This expansion in the population tends to increase the level and scope of the demand for consumer goods. However, it is a demographic fact that the poor reproduce at a much faster rate than do the rich. Second, the wealthy tend to be somewhat more conservative in making large-scale investments in new, as yet untested, areas of potential economic growth. It is more difficult for the wealthy to shift their large accumulations of capital into and out of boom industries than it is for those with smaller and less complicated "portfolios." Finally, the service income of the poor tends to be greater, in absolute terms, than that of the rich. The incentive "to get rich" is much greater for the poor than it is for the rich. This is particularly true for investment profits. For these reasons, the share of wealth held by the top five or ten percent of the population has, he argued, tended to show no increase over time. That is, the wealthy do not tend to get wealthier, in relative terms, as development occurs; rather, they tend to stay wealthy in absolute terms. Conversely, the less wealthy tend to increase both their absolute and relative shares of the societal product—thus accounting for decreasing levels of inequality at higher levels of development. Much of the confusion is seated in whether preindustrial as well as industrial development is considered.

In 1963, Kuznets published a more detailed study of this question which was based upon a fuller, although still undernourished, set of data. Three basic conclusions were offered: (1) the distribution of income is more unequal in the less developed countries (LDCs) than in the developed nations; (2) the inequality of wealth in the developed countries (DCs) has decreased over time; and (3) the patterns of income distribution in LDCs is very similar to the corresponding patterns of the DCs at an earlier stage of growth (1963:68). Thus, he buttresses the arguments made in his 1955 presidential address to the American Economic Association in two important ways. The newly reported empirical findings are consonant with the earlier arguments. Further, Kuznets recognized the difficulty in inferring a process model from cross-sectional results, however scanty. Accordingly, the 1963 article reports some longitudinal data which offers evidence that the cross-sectional and longitudinal pictures are basically similar.

Having outlined and examined these two facets of the dual economy theory and their implications for the distribution of material product, Kuznets speculated about the non-economic aspects of the relationship:

[55]

Hence we may conclude that the major offset to the widening of income inequality associated with the shift from agriculture and the countryside to industry and the city must have been a rise in the income share of the lower groups within the non-agricultural sector of the population.... Much is to be said for the notion that once the early turbulent phases of industrialization and urbanization had passed, a variety of forces converged to bolster the economic position of the lower-income groups within the urban population. The very fact that after a while, an increasing proportion of the urban population was "native," i.e., born in cities rather than in the rural areas, and hence more able to take advantage of the possibilities of city life in preparation for the economic struggle, meant a better chance for organization and adaptation, a better basis for securing greater income shares than was possible for the newly "immigrant" population coming from the countryside or from abroad. The increasing efficiency of the older, established urban population should also be taken into account. Furthermore, in democratic societies the growing political power of the urban lower-income groups led to a variety of protective and supporting legislation, much of it aimed to counteract the worst effects of rapid industrialization and urbanization and to support the claims of the broad masses for more adequate shares of the growing income of the country [1963:17].

Kuznets' arguments may be represented by the two aforementioned hypotheses: (1) that the rich tend to save more than the poor, and (2) that new wealth tends to accumulate in industrial, urban areas. When coupled with the enabling assumption that developed countries have tended to experience rapid increases in urbanization during economic growth, this leads to the deduced hypothesis that inequality of wealth tends to increase at early stages of growth and to decrease at later stages. This suggestion is appropriate across the wide range of variation from preindustrial economic structures to highly developed industrial ones, but may not be highly salient within tightly restricted ranges. As the above quote illustrates, it is not suggested that this "increase then decrease" hypothesis is valid within the more limited range of modern development.

Kuznets' arguments have proven somewhat difficult to untangle. If developmental experience ranging from preindustrial hunting and farming to highly industrialized modern economies is considered, one would expect an initial decrease in equality to occur up to industrialization, although thereafter, declining inequality would be associated with increased development. The overall picture from preindustrial to industrial development is one of increased, then decreased inequality. However, all of Kuznets' evidence is garnered from the developmental

[56]

experience of industrializing countries. Many scholars (*inter alios,* Adelman and Morris, 1967) have interpreted the inverted-U hypothesis to be applicable to the industrial period itself. The position taken in this study, which deals with modern development (i.e., postindustrial revolution), is that there is a curvilinear positive relationship hypothesized by Kuznets which relates increasing levels of development and equality. It is this hypothesis that presents the basic curvilinear relationship which is hypothesized between inequality and growth. It must be pointed out at this juncture that this curvilinearity is not so much a function of the relationship itself as the result of the implicit though unspecified effects of political mobilization and participation as well as governmental policy which occur at the higher levels of development.

Gehard Lenski (1966) has addressed the question of development and inequality from a historical-sociological perspective. Basically, he argues that as a society moves from simple hunting and gathering modes of economic production to an agrarian mode, there is an increase in the accumulation of wealth by individals and groups of individuals which in turn causes an increase in the inequality within that society. However, as the mode of production changes from agricultural to industrial, inequality begins progressively to lessen. Lenski's theory is similar in its conclusions to that of Kuznets: both posit a curvilinear relationship between development and inequality—though for somewhat different reasons. Phillips Cutright (1967) used Lenski's ideas to structure an empirical test of this hypothesis. Cutright's analysis did offer empirical evidence somewhat more substantial than was used to support Kuznets' idea that nations with high levels of development tend to have less inequality than do nations at lower levels of development.

Adelman and Morris (1967,1973) have written two books which examine this question from yet another, largely atheoretical, perspective. They are not so much interested in explaining inequality as statistically defining and describing the characteristics of the highly equal and unequal societies. To do this, a large data base of qualitatively scored sociopolitical as well as more conventional economic indicators for a sample of some seventy nations in the 1960s is used. The statistical technique they employ is a form of discriminant analysis developed by Morgan and Sondquist (1967) which is known as AID (Automatic Interaction Detector). Without going into the technical aspects of this inductive, variance-partitioning technique, suffice it to say that there are severe questions about its applicability to samples of seventy inasmuch as it was designed for large surveys with sample size approaching three-thousand. However, Adelman and Morris feel that they are examining the same curvilinear hypothesis discussed above—though they call it the "inverted-U" hypothesis. Their overall conclusion is that there is "no basis in fact" for the optimistic hypothesis which related equality to high levels of development. Specifically, they note:

> Our analysis indicates that the relationship between level of economic development and the income share of the poorest 60 percent of the population is asymmetrically U-shaped. Both extreme economic underdevelopment and high levels of economic development are associated with greater income equality; between the extremes a more equal income distribution is generally associated with a lower level of development [1973:186].

Their interpretation is that the analysis supports (1) Kuznets and Myrdal, each of whom, they assert, argued that the poorest groups' shares of income have tended to decrease with growth, and (2) the dual economy arguments offered by Baran (1958). However, in addition to the technical flaws in their work, they part company with Kuznets' theoretical position, prior to his examination of the patterns of saving and wealth accumulation. Additionally, they draw no distinction between preindustrial and industrial development patterns, although their data is drawn from the latter set. Thus, while they would assert the contrary, it seems that their study actually may contradict the arguments and analysis of Kuznets. Ranis, while praising this work by Adelman and Morris as exploratory, also criticizes it as jumping to conclusions.

> Adelman and Morris do occasionally move to thin ice ... [when] ... associations or clusters lead them to the Marxist view on the relation between economic structure, distribution, and political structure ... especially when they conclude that agricultural productivity increase does not matter for income distribution—an especially untenable proposition based on static non-causal evidence [1975:562].

Robert Jackman (1975) has attempted to focus both on the politics and the economics of social equality. For some purposes, his analysis is similar to the present one. He starts with the same building block

[58]

which began this study: development. Based upon much of the same work discussed above, he posits and tests the curvilinear hypothesis. The countries he uses in his sample are all noncommunist economies from the early to mid-1960s and number about sixty. Using a Schutz coefficient of income equality, an index of the experience with social security programs, and a measure of the extent of social welfare in a country, he employs multiple regression analysis to test the differences between linear, polynomial, and logarithmic specifications between the level of development and the level of equality in his sample. Because of the similarity between Jackman's work and this study, his results will be explored in greater detail below by way of comparison and contrast to the results generated through the empirical test that follows. In summary, Jackman found an extremely good fit between either of the specified forms of curvilinearity (i.e., second-order polynomial and logarithmic) and the level of social equality. Thus, his work lends much support toward this basic hypothesis that development decreases inequality.

The discussion of the research into this question could go on almost interminably because the problem of equality has proved to be extremely intriguing from a wide spectrum of viewpoints, ranging from the desire to improve the lot of man through policy questions of how effectively to do it to the purely theoretical fascination with the concept of equality itself. This review ends with consideration of the works of Hollis Chenery and associates, since these works represent one of the most recent, systematic, and ambitious analyses of this topic. The first volume produced by the project headed by Chenery under the auspices of the World Bank, *Redistribution with Growth,* has two primary facets. The first part consists of a cross-sectional test of the relationship between development as measured by *per capita* GNP and the relative shares of income possessed by the top twenty, middle forty, and bottom forty percent of the population. One strong contribution has been made by this project in amassing data on income shares (Jain, 1975) through combining and collating survey and other data from a large number of case studies of specific countries.

The basic argument offered in this work is in part a refutation of the Marxist-structuralist proposition that growth tends to hinder the redistribution of wealth. The cross-sectional evidence shows strong confirmation of the Kuznets argument: the relative income share of the top twenty percent of the population (i.e., the rich) is reduced at a diminishing rate as the level of development is increased and the relative income share of the bottom forty percent (i.e., the poor) is increased, again at a diminishing rate, by higher levels of development.

The second phase of this important work not only includes policy relevant and therefore manipulable variables such as educational level, but also examines the social and political aspects of society in developing nations through rather detailed case studies of several individual states such as India and South Korea. In summary to the first half of the effort, the World Bank authors report the conclusion that Kuznets' original hypothesis is supported and that, contrary to the Marxist argument, "[t]he cross-section evidence does not support the view that a high rate of economic growth has an adverse effect upon relative equality" (1974:17).

Summarizing the second part of their effort, they find that policy variables do have a positive impact upon the distribution of income and that the political as well as social aspects of development planning are extremely important. The first part of their analysis is much more comprehensive, integrated, systematic, and thorough than the latter, however, and much work is still to be done on the noneconomic aspects of this problem.

The companion volume, *Patterns of Development: 1950-1970*, analyzes the patterns of development over time, but because of the unavailability of time-series income distribution data, it reports only the analysis contained in the earlier volume. There is, however, a strong contribution which this volume, as well as earlier work by Chenery and Taylor (1968), makes. By pooling cross-sectional and longitudinal data they are able to obtain evidence on whether the cross-sectional and the longitudinal analyses of development exhibit any significant differences. In short, do inferences from cross-sectional analyses of development bear any relationship to the ones we would draw from more process-oriented longitudinal analyses? With some qualifications, the answer to this question is basically "yes." In general, they found that the longitudinal processes involving development such as saving, capital, and trade transformation are well reflected by the static analysis. In their words:

In evaluating these results we have generally adopted the customary interpretation that cross-section results reflect a long-term adjustment and time-series estimates [reflect] a short or partial adjustment to change in the exogenous variables [1968:134].

[60]

This contribution is extremely significant not because it gives license for the use of static analysis for process models—that is clearly a misinterpretation. Rather, it does help eliminate one criticism which might invalidate many studies of and related to development; namely, that the process of development is grossly misrepresented by static analysis using various levels of development as surrogates for the process itself. Beyond that, it is still possible that the relationship between the process of development and other processes, such as income redistribution for example, is not accurately reflected by cross-sectional surrogates.

The analyses discussed above are not exhaustive. Nonetheless, they do give much support to the curvilinear hypothesis from a host of perspectives, ranging from the theoretical to the descriptive on the one hand, and across the multidisciplinary spectrum of social science on the other. This enhances the validity of choosing to begin with this foundation. What follows is a reexamination of the curvilinear hypothesis with a more exhaustive and contemporary sample of countries, as well as a different, and hopefully improved indicator of inequality which was developed in the previous chapter.

The operationalization of the economic development of a polity rejects the most conventional indicator, Gross National Product (GNP). Several reasons temper this judgment. First, GNP has been criticized by many social scientists as being too aggregate in nature and thus oversimplifying the complexity of any economic structure, and as being pro-Western and procapitalist in its biases. Moreover, since this study includes economies of all types, ranging from capitalist to socialist and communist, national income is problematic, since strictly speaking it is not comparable across economic systems. Energy consumption *per capita* is utilized in this study as the operational indicator of the level of development. It is related to, but not isomorphic with, national income. Not only is it directly comparable across all types of economic systems, but also it gives an aggregate picture of the (direct and indirect) delivery of economic goods and services to the "average" individual within that society.

Three specifications of the relationship between development and inequality are formalized and estimated using the referent data set. The discussion above argues that on the basis of theoretical expectations this relationship should be curvilinear. Yet, the implicit benchmark for such a formalization is the linear hypothesis. In addition to the linear benchmark, two curvilinear forms are offered.

The first of these is logarithmic, while the second is second-order polynomial.

There are two theoretical differences between these specifications. The logarithmic form mathematically attempts, in this case, to approximate a threshold argument that as development proceeds to higher levels, the corresponding decrements in inequality tend to get smaller and approach minimal levels. This means that there may be an absolute limit to a nation's ability to decrease inequality through economic growth. The polynomial specification argues that not only is there a limit to the ability of a nation to decrease inequality through increasing its economic prosperity, but also that after a limit is reached, increasing inequality tends to be associated with increases in growth. The second major distinction between the curvilinear hypotheses concerns the size of the response in inequality associated with various levels of development. The logarithmic form embodies a steep decline toward the limit, while the slope of the curvilinear form is more gradual. This last distinction is particularly important because it results in two different implications for the very poor countries: the logarithmic form predicts rapid—almost immediate—payoffs to increases in the level of development. On the other hand, the polynomial form suggests a more deferred "payoff scheme." These three specifications are represented by the following set of equations:

$$(3.1) \quad Y = \alpha + \beta X1$$

$$(3.2) \quad Y = \alpha + \beta(\ln_e X1)$$

$$(3.3) \quad Y = \alpha + \beta_1 X1 + \beta_2 X1^2$$

Where: Y = Inequality index
$X1$ = Energy comsumption *per capita*.

Before proceeding to the data analysis, two brief words of caution must prevail. First, for any statistical test to be valid, the assumptions that underlie that test must not be violated. In the case of the classical normal linear model (OLS) there are five such assumptions: the error terms are (1) distributed normally; (2) have a mean of zero; (3) have equal variance over the entire range of variation in independent variables (homoscedasticity); and (4) are not serially or cross-sectionally correlated with one another. The fifth assumption deals not with the error term, but concerns the variance in the independent variables.

Specifically, this assumption states that the independent variables must be nonstochastic. Accordingly, the covariation in the independent variables must be observable and measurable over the entire range of variation in the dependent variables.[2]

Extremely important among the many implications of these assumptions is that the model that is being evaluated through this classical normal linear regression technique is complete, nonredundant, and properly specified. That is, no important variables are left out, no extraneous ones are included, and among the remaining dependent and independent variables all of the interrelationships are correctly specified. Few analyses can pass such scrutiny. The present effort is no exception. However, in practice it is possible to relax each of the assumptions without completely invalidating the technique, and palliatives exist for situations in which any particular assumption seems grossly violated. For the most part, the consequences of this sort of statistical meddling, called econometrics by some, are the weakening of the strength of the tests which are being conducted.

The second overriding word of caution is nestled in the fact that even when all of the assumptions appear to have been reasonably fulfilled, regression results may be extremely misleading unless the original scatterplots as well as the residuals are carefully studied in their own right. The mathematical and statistical analysis of residuals has long been advocated if not required by econometric theory and practice. Their visual inspection and the role of graphic representations of the original data have received considerably less attention. Edward Tufte's voice has been one of the most persistent in advocating the analysis of scatterplots and residuals as a necessary part of data analysis (1970, 1974). Anscombe (1973) has provided a striking example of why this is true by constructing four different sets of data which across sets have the identical mean for each of the variables, the same regression equation, the same coefficient of determination, and the same estimate of the standard error of the slope estimate. Without examining the scatterplot and residuals one would never discover the "substantive" uniqueness of each data set. One set represents a robust linear relationship, another is curvilinear, a third is strongly skewed by one single outlier, and the fourth is virtually without variation on the independent variable. Thus, for the purposes of this and following chapters, the analysis of residuals and scatterplots will be an integral part of the data analysis.

However, since the model which will eventually be tested is to result in part from earlier analyses of modules and is consequently at this stage known to be underspecified, the statistical but not visual analysis of residuals will be held in abeyance until a more definitive version is itself tested. Prior to that stage of analysis the residuals themselves will be treated as theoretically meaningful in the sense that they contain variation yet to be explained by modules not presently incorporated into the overall model.

Figure 3.1 presents the scattergram of the level of development as measured by per capita energy consumption against the inequality index. Additionally, each of the estimated equations, (3.1) through (3.3), is plotted against the original inequality index. Table 3.1 summarizes the statistical information that results from the OLS estimates of these three equations.

TABLE 3.1. *Regression of Inequality Index on the Level of Development via Linear (3.1), Logarithmic (3.2), and Polynomial (3.3) Specifications* [a]

	Dependent Variable : Inequality Index		
INDEPENDENT VARIABLE	REGRESSION COEFFICIENT	STANDARD ERROR	STANDARDIZED COEFFICIENT
Equation (3.1)			
ENGCON	−25.12*	1.83	−.79
Equation (3.2)			
LNENGCON	−.29*	.02	−.75
Equation (3.3)			
ENGCON	−44.65*	4.09	−1.40
ENGCONSQ	276.85*	53.13	.67

Equation	R2	$\overline{R2}$	F	P=	N
(3.1)	.62	.62	187.68	.000	114
(3.2)	.57	.57	150.12	.000	114
(3.3)	.70	.69	128.94	.000	113

a. Where: ENGCON   = Energy consumption per capita (X1)
           LNENGCON = Natural logarithm of ENGCON ($\ln_e X1$)
           ENGCONSQ = Energy consumption squared ($X1^2$)
A more complete explanation of these variables is given in Appendix B.
* Estimate is statistically significant at the 0.05 level, or better.

FIGURE 3.1. The Relationship between Inequality and the Level of Economic Development as Measured by Energy Consumption *Per Capita*

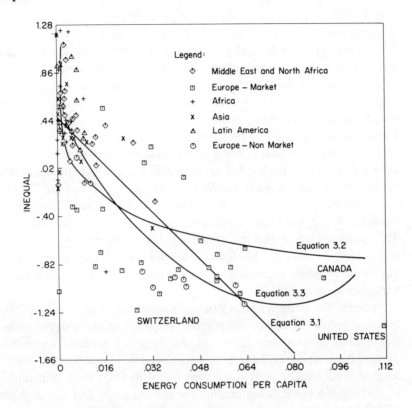

Turning first to the scattergram, several prominent features of the data are revealed. The distribution of polities is highly concentrated at the low end of the development scale. This is consonant with many portraits which divide the global actors into "different developmental worlds." That is, a few nations are relatively well developed while the bulk of the nations in the international system are highly undeveloped. The outliers on the high end of this distribution tend to be Western, industrial powers such as the United States, Canada, and Switzerland, as indicated in Figure 3.1.

While this type of skewed distribution of the level of development across global actors may be descriptively accurate, it does indicate a violation of one of the OLS assumptions. Specifically, the level of development as measured here represents a stochastic explanatory variable in that the number of observations at the low end of the scale will tend to "overpower" the relatively few observations which represent highly developed nations.[3] Also, it is impossible to determine whether the few cases at the high end of the distribution, e.g., the United States, are statistically representative of the unobserved cases which may exist only hypothetically. Moreover, the distribution of inequality is also shown to be greatly skewed in that there are a great many more societies which exhibit high levels of inequality than ones which have a relatively egalitarian distribution of social product. Furthermore, the main outliers on each of these two scales are the United States and Canada. The confluence of the skewed nature of the distribution of both the level of development and the level of inequality results in a scattergram suggestive of the "two world" *Weltanschauung*. First, there is a large number of highly populated, poor societies which have an inegalitarian distribution of social product. This group may be called the "poor cousins." The other group, "the rich cousins," considerably fewer in number, has a somewhat higher degree of variation in economic development and a lesser degree of variation in inequality.

By itself, the scattergram is strongly supportive of the negative link between inequality and development. Inequality tends to decrease as the level of development increases. As there are no societies in the present data set which have both a low level of inequality and a low level of development, neither are there any with a high level of inequality and a high level of development. The curvilinearity which is posited to reflect the form of this negative relationship is not made grossly implausible by this scatterplot. Visually, there appears to be a two-faceted threshold in effect. The large cluster of cases in the high inequality-low development section of the plot space suggests that historically there has been much difficulty in the progression of societies from low toward high levels of both development and equality.

Theoretically, this bolsters the argument that in the absence of a sizable portion of economic product to distribute, it is extremely difficult to talk about the existence of relatively high levels of equality in a polity. The doublebind is that apparently after a certain level of equality is established, presumably due in large part to a higher level of development, it is very difficult for a society to make additional advances in decreasing levels of inequality via increasingly higher levels of development.

As suggested earlier, the regional variation in the level of inequality seems largely conditioned by the link between development and inequality. African and Asian countries, comprising the bulk of the Third and Fourth Worlds, typically have low levels of economic development and high degrees of inequality. On the other hand, the Western European nations, irrespective of market orientation, have uniformly lower inequality levels and higher levels of development. Thus, when the level of development is considered, little difference exists between the capitalist and communist countries—as indicated by their close proximity in Figure 3.1.

Visually, it is virtually impossible to evaluate anything more than the general appropriateness of each of the three equations to the actual data set. None of these formulations seems grossly inappropriate. Prior to interpretation of the statistical evidence which is aimed at providing greater information about the relative appropriateness of each, several points need be noted. First, the large "clump" of cases which represents the "poor cousins" tends to lower the mean of both distributions. This, in turn, will tend to produce regression results which are "forced" through this group. The slope of the regression lines, once anchored in this clump, can relatively easily be influenced by a small number of cases which may cluster at the other end of the distribution (e.g., the United States and Canada). Also, this clump tends to increase the high coefficients of determination, since so many of the observations lie near the means of both of the distributions.

Furthermore, it will be very difficult to distinguish between the three equations inasmuch as (1) they are all very similar at the lower ranges of variation (i.e., are highly correlated); (2) most of the available data are clustered at these low ranges; and (3) the two cases that represent the high extreme of the independent variable tend to have an exaggerated influence in determining the exact shape of the line(s) at the upper bounds. That is, do the United States and Canada, among others, accurately represent the other unmeasured cases of high development and high equality? Further, since it appears that the explanatory variable is in fact stochastic, the parameter estimates themselves will not be the Best Linear Unbiased Estimates (BLUE). Unfortunately, very little can be done about this problem. One "solution" is to examine the linearity via a transformation of the underlying distribution which will

[67]

artificially spread the distribution over a less or more concentrated interval. Also, one might question the linearity in the parameters themselves. However, without theoretically compelling reasons, either solution may be inappropriate, inasmuch as a transformation of either sort can be "discovered" which will ply the data in whatsoever fashion is desired. Such a strategy will stand very little chance of disconfirmation. Thus, no such transformations will be proposed, and the residuals will be interpreted—as previously suggested—as discrepancies from the proposed model which are themselves theoretically meaningful. The parameter estimates will be viewed as tentative, and the inflation in the $\overline{R2}$s will be duly noted.

As shown in Table 3.1, each regression produced markedly similar results. Each of the three equations explained more than half of the total variation in inequality reflected in the present data set. All of the various regression coefficients are statistically significant, and consequently, so are the F-tests for the overall significance of each line. The estimated functional forms are also very similar—especially at the medium-to-low end of the development scale. As expected, the $\overline{R2}$s are robust, since each regression line is forced through the cluster of low equality, low development societies. Consequently, there is very little statistical evidence for choosing one estimated solution as more appropriate than another. For example, it is clear that each of the three equations taken separately offers a substantial amount of evidence for three different hypotheses. It should also be clear that the $\overline{R2}$s ought not be used to winnow solutions in this particular case.

What can be concluded from the examination of the scattergram and the regression results is that the negative nature of the link between these two phenomena is consistent with the data set. Even granting the acknowledged statistical problems and consequent artifacts, the negative link solutions are each very robust. Further, the curvilinear form of this negative hypothesis is not refuted and seems plausible. In summary, two requirements are summoned by the nature of the evidence presented so far: (1) additional evaluation of evidence accumulated by others, notably Jackman, and (2) while the general hypothesis is not refuted, the choice of the most appropriate specific form, for a host of reasons, will be made on the basis of theoretical information as much as statistical and visual evidence.

The outstanding work of Jackman can help provide additional empir-

TABLE 3.2. *Regression of Jackman's Schutz Coefficient of Income Inequality on the Level of Development via Linear (3.11), Logarithmic (3.21), and Polynomial (3.31) Specifications* [a]

	Dependent Variable : Inequality Index		
INDEPENDENT VARIABLE	**REGRESSION COEFFICIENT**	**STANDARD ERROR**	**STANDARDIZED COEFFICIENT**
Equation (3.21)			
Energy cons.	$-.0044^*$	$.0008^*$	$-.60$
Equation (3.22)			
Natural log. Energy cons.	-5.55^*	$.89$	$-.63$
Equation (3.23)			
Energy cons.	$-.0086^*$	$.0018$	-1.18
Energy cons. squared	$.74E^{-6*}$ [b]	$.3E^{-6}$	$.63$

Equation	R2	$\overline{R2}$ [c]	F	P=	N
(3.21)	.36	—	32.74	.000	60
(3.22)	.40	—	38.64	.000	60
(3.23)	.42	.40	20.91	.000	60

a. Adapted from Jackman (1975, pp. 37–39). In order to facilitate comparison, the signs of relationship have been changed, since the Schutz coefficient is scaled inversely to the inequality index used in this study.
b. Exponential notation: multiply the number to the left of the "E" by ten raised to the number to the right of the "E".
c. Not presented in Jackman (1974).
* Estimate is statistically significant at the 0.05 level, or better.

ical evidence when examined more closely than the brief summary presented above. Table 3.2 presents the regression results from his study, which are comparable to those presented in Table 3.1. Thus, equations (3.21) through (3.23) are respectively equivalent in form to equations (3.1) through (3.3), which are presented above. One difference is that Jackman's dependent variable is a Schutz coefficient of sector income equality, as opposed to the index which is developed and used in this study. Further, his data, which consist of a sample of sixty noncommunist polities, are taken from the year 1960. Consequently, when comparing the two sets of results it is virtually impossible to uncover the extent of change in the aggregate relationship between inequality and development which might possibly have occurred in the decade since Jackman's data were collected, while at the same time uncovering the nature of that relationship itself.

If however, his results are found to be substantially similar to those of the present study, which in fact they are, then one might argue one or both of two major points. First, it would seem that if the two studies were uncovering a random relationship, it would be unlikely for both to reveal highly similar nonrandom patterns—unless they were driven by the same artifact. Moreover, if there is indeed some important relationship which Jackman demonstrated with the smaller, 1960-based data set, then if the much more extensive 1970-based data reveal the same relationship, it is unlikely that the relationship itself has changed greatly over time—although the position of individual observations may have changed markedly. This does not contradict the notion that, in this case, the cross-sectional aggregate evidence is a moderately adequate characterization of the longitudinal process involved.

In fact, Jackman's results are similar to the present study's, though important distinctions do exist and will be discussed below. While the total variation explained by equations (3.21) through (3.23) is considerably less than in the counterpart equations evaluated in this study (e.g., .36 compared to .62), Jackman's OLS estimates are robust and significant in all parameters. Furthermore, the standardized coefficients for each of the two sets of three equations are virtually identical. For example, if one compares $-.60$ to $-.79$, $-.63$ to $-.75$, -1.18 to -1.4, and .63 to .67, not only are the magnitudes of the coefficients consistent across sets of equations, but also the internal relationships within any given set are themselves preserved.

On the basis of his results, Jackman argues that the curvilinear forms provide a significantly better fit than does the linear form on the basis that the coefficient of the square term in equation (3.2) should not be significant if the linear model is correct. In both his data and those presented here, the square term is significant, thus implying the inadequacy of the linear model. However, in both his study and this one, the United States and Canada are outliers. In fact, his scattergram looks almost identical in form to Figure 3.2. The implication is that if the United States and Canada were removed as "deviant" cases, the linear form would be most "correct" in the sense that it would provide the best fit.

While Jackman does not go into the problem of stochastic explanatory variables, nor does he consider deviant case analysis, there are theoretical reasons which suggest that these two observations should remain in the analysis. These reasons hinge upon two considerations. First is the assumption that the United States and Canada are fairly representative of the unmeasured observations at the high end of the development scale; second is that the United States and Canada to a lesser extent are both viewed by many policy makers in the less developed polities as representing goals toward which they are striving. In short, to Jackman's conclusion that the linear model should be rejected, one must append several caveats about the nature of the underlying distribution of the explanatory variables as well as the residuals. The likelihood of each of these aforementioned caveats being valid in this particular case should perhaps soften his categorical rejection of the linear hypothesis.

Briefly, Jackman argues that either the logarithmic or the polynomial form seems statistically appropriate (i.e., significant). His choice between the two curvilinear functions is based more on visual, epistemological, and theoretical grounds, none of which played a part in his rejection of the linear hypothesis, than on statistical grounds:

> In other words, on visual grounds, it might be argued that the logarithmic model conforms more closely with the general pattern of the data with its steep initial curve which tends to level off at higher stages of economic development. Finally, the criterion of parsimony implies that the logarithmic specification is preferable to the polynomial because it is simpler [bivariate rather than multivariate], and is not clearly inferior in terms of goodness of fit ... [and] ... retaining two highly collinear exogenous variables ... serves to introduce unnecessary complications [1975:39-43].

As evidenced by the above statement, Jackman does not base his choice of the logarithmic model on statistical evidence gleaned from the various regressions. It is argued here that the choice of appropriate forms must, in this case, be made upon theoretical grounds. The bulk of the theories invoked both here and in Jackman suggest a curvilinear form which more closely approximates the logarithmic one. If that logarithmic form seems theoretically most appropriate and the data do not lend themselves to a refutation of it, then most of what could possibly be accomplished in the data analysis—which after all is nonexperimental evidence—will have been accomplished. That is, did the data analysis provide a test of the hypothesis, and secondly did the test suggest that the hypothesis was incorrect? With this type of interpretation both Jackman's evidence and that presented here suggest the viability of the logarithmic, curvilinear form.

[71]

However, it is possible for virtually any of the proposed forms to be "correct." Since there are relatively few observations at the high end of the development scale, one can posit any potential distribution of cases which, if measured, would support any of the three equations (3.1) through (3.3). The reasons for adopting the logarithmic form, it should be stressed, are based upon the theoretical arguments presented above as well as the statistical evidence garnered from the scatterplots and regressions. Thus, while Jackman's conclusions are much the same as those reached here, it is felt that a more rigorous and substantial evaluation was conducted in the present study, and as such not only bolsters, but significantly adds to the findings of the earlier work.

3.3 THE EFFECTS OF RAPID GROWTH AND DIVERSITY

The previous section offers theoretical and empirical arguments that seek to establish the link between the level of development that characterizes a polity and the distribution of social product which exists within it. Arguments based on this and other studies were also surveyed, and they suggested that the underlying process of "moving along" the developmental ladder or scale is related to movement along the inequality ladder. Further, the relationship between these two processes itself was argued to be captured by the nature of the cross-sectional evidence. The underlying assumption of all of these arguments is based upon the transformation of the different levels of development into different levels of equality. Stated another way, in assuming that the aggregate cross-sectional model is an accurate characterization of the underlying process, one builds in the second-order effects which translate changes in the level of development into changes in the level of inequality.

Substantively, this section attempts to make explicit these assumptions about the nature of the mechanisms which at the same time preserve the relationship between the level of development and inequality as well as build in the dynamics which relate the changes in each of these variables to one another. This will be accomplished through the consideration of two factors, the diversity of the economic structure and short-term economic growth, and their subsequent incorporation into a more complete model relating the development process to inequality.

[72]

As with most social phenomenon, there are at least two contradictory schools of thought about this "translation." One school of thought is presented by Lenski (1966), who contends that increases in economic growth themselves lead directly toward concomitant increases in equality. That is, both the level of economic development (first-order effects) and the rate of growth (second-order effects) are positively related to increases in equality. The countervening argument also has many adherents (*viz.*, Olson, 1963). It is based upon the assumption that rapid economic growth tends to displace economic product in the short-run in such a fashion as to increase the overall inequality. More specifically, drawing upon the arguments advanced by Kuznets and presented above, it appears at least equally likely that rapid growth will tend to redistribute the labor force at a faster rate than the population can restructure its composition by differential reproduction and migration. Consequently, in the short-run there will be an accumulation of product into new sectors—urban and industrial—which tends to increase the overall inequality. Furthermore, the initial capital benefit of an expanding economic system will be more substantial for the wealthy with diverse investments, since payoffs to the newest entrants require a certain amount of time before materializing. In addition, a great many more small-scale ventures will fail than succeed. All of these factors tend to strengthen the relative position of the already wealthy *vis-a-vis* the less wealthy.

It must be remembered, of course, that these are second-order effects which are mostly of short-term significance in an expanding economy. The aggregate level mechanisms outlined and tested in the previous section are not incompatible with these causal effects, which on the surface may seem to contradict the earlier arguments. Rather, the second-order effects are simply different than the first-order ones. Jackman (1975) attempts to incorporate this rate argument into his model by use of a measure of inflation. Empirically, he finds little evidence in his data to support the hypothesis that growth tends to increase inequality. Thus, he concludes that while the data do not support the hypothesis, the theoretical arguments are far more compelling than his disconfirmation, and he puts the matter aside—presumably for future research.

While certainly analytically plausible, the assertion of the hypothesis that rapid growth leads to increased inequality does on the surface contradict the notion that the higher the level of development, the greater will be the equality. If one is to adopt both of these hypoth-

[73]

eses, it is imperative to present the mechanism(s) which not only map growth into the level of development but also translate the relationship between the effects of growth and inequality from positive to negative. Since the diversity of the economic structure represents one of the major stated goals of economic policy in many Third World countries which are viewed as developing—ranging from oil-rich, single-commodity economies such as Iran to less wealthy and less concentrated economies such as India—it seems plausible that diversity itself may be a mediating factor in the relationship between growth and the level of development and, in turn, the level of equality.

Early work focuses upon varied aspects of diversity which may accompany development and thereby affect the patterns of distribution. Kravis (1960), for example, has studied the composition of the labor force during various stages of industrialization. The general conclusion he reaches is that there is a marked tendency of developing nations to exhibit increasing levels of labor differentiation. The implication is that the process which Kuznets and Myrdal each described for an entire economy may also occur within those sectors of the economy which benefit most from growth. Within the urban and industrializing sectors, one may expect increasing inequality during the early stages of growth due to the increasing differentiation of the labor mass. Certain professions and industries will prosper and flourish, while others will find their utility declining in the new, industrial sectors.

It is argued here that while rapid economic growth tends to increase inequality in the short-run; if, however, that rapid growth is channeled through an economy which is either already diversified or is diversifying during the process of industrialization, then the overall effect of the interaction of these two factors will be a tendency for inequality to decrease. Specifically, the relationship between growth and inequality is positive, but the interaction of rapid growth and the diversity of the economic structure have an opposite effect. The two hypotheses may be formalized as follows:

(3.4) $Y = \alpha + \beta_{42} X2$

(3.5) $Y = \alpha + \beta_{53} X2 \cdot X3$

Where: Y = Inequality index
$X2$ = Index of construction activity
$X3$ = Index of economic diversity

[74]

While the inequality index was constructed in the previous chapter, two empirical indices must be derived before these two equations can be evaluated and incorporated into the larger model. Construction activity is often taken as a bellwether of the trend of the economy and is itself an important aspect of economic planning because it involves so many interrelated facets of an economic structure—labor, capital, and growth. Further, it tends to enhance the overall economic picture because activity in this industry spreads to a myriad of related industrial and agricultural endeavors, such as concrete and steel production, lumber, transportation, and ultimately consumer services. An index of this type of activity was taken from a United Nations report, *Yearbook of Construction Statistics* 1963-1972 (1974). A full explanation of the index is provided therein. Basically, it has two characteristics that are of importance here. First, it is an indicator of short-term economic growth, particularly in construction, which can provide a transforming "boost" to an economy. Second, it is a longitudinally measured index in which one polity's performance is compared to its past performance rather than to the performance of other polities. What is comparable across polities is their longitudinal performance in increasing or decreasing short-term economic growth as reflected in the index of construction activity. This index will be used in evaluating equations (3.4) and (3.5).

The index used to assess the diversity of the economic structure is based upon an index of concentration developed by Herfindal (1950) and used by many other researchers (Ray and Singer, 1974). It attempts to measure the extent to which the possession of some quantity is concentrated in a system. The measure of diversity uses the concentration index to measure the extent of concentration of the work force within any given sector of the economy and the concentration of Gross Domestic Product (GDP) which is generated within any given sector. Since diversity, not concentration, is the area of concern here, each of these two indices have been subtracted from unity, so that high scores reflect high amounts of diversity. The final index of diversity is the ratio of diversity in the work force to the diversity in the generation of GDP.

The index embodies the argument that an economy is diversified to the extent that the net product generated comes from a wide variety of economic activities which themselves are not highly concentrated in any particular sector. In such a diverse economic structure, the work

[75]

force will be evenly distributed across different types of economic activity, ranging from industrial to agricultural. This index, called DIVERSITY, is given by the following formulas:

$$\text{DIVERSITY} = \frac{1 - \text{WFCONC}}{1 - \text{GDPCONC}}$$

Where:

$$\text{WFCONC} = \sum_{i=1}^{N} \text{WF}_i^2$$

$$\text{GDPCONC} = \sum_{i=1}^{N} \text{GDP}_i^2$$

$\text{WF}_i = $ Portion of Total Work Force in Sector i

$\text{GDP}_i = $ Portion of Total Gross Domestic Product Generated within Sector i

$N = $ Number of sectors

The advantage of this index over many other indices of diversity is that it does not necessarily give higher scores to more developed or wealthy nations. Rather, cast in its ratio form, it is used to compare the balance in the diversity of both large and small economies. Computationally, it is similar to a Gini index of sector income inequality.

Armed with these two indices it is empirically possible to evaluate equations (3.4) and (3.5). However, since one variable, the level of development, has already been built into the model, it is more appropriate to evaluate the model using these two new variables and their interactions. Thus, in relation to the level of development, the growth and diversity variables are herein viewed as complementary rather than competing. Equation (3.6) presents the mathematical form of this expanded model:

(3.6) $\quad Y = \alpha + \beta_{61}X1 + \beta_{62}X2 + \beta_{63}X3 \cdot X2$

Where: $\quad Y = $ Inequality index
$\quad X1 = $ Energy consumption *per capita*
$\quad X2 = $ Index of construction activity
$\quad X3 = $ Index of economic diversity

TABLE 3.3. *Regression of Inequality Index on the Level of Development, Index of Short-Term Economic Activity, and the Diversity of the Economic Structure as It Mediates Short-Term Activity*[a]

| | Dependent Variable : | Inequality Index | |
INDEPENDENT VARIABLE	REGRESSION COEFFICIENT	STANDARD ERROR	STANDARDIZED COEFFICIENT
LNENGCON	−.27*	.04	−.69
IXCONS	.005*	.003	.43
INTERACT	−1.61*	68	−.44

R^2	$\overline{R^2}$	F	P−
.621	.603	22.47	.000

a. Where: LNENGCON = Logarithm of Energy Consumption per Capita, $(\ln_e X1)$
           IXCONS = Index of Short Term Economic Growth, (X)
           INTERACT = Interaction of IXCONS (X2) and the Diversity of the Economic Structure (X3)
  A more complete explanation of these variables is given in Appendix B.
* Estimate is statistically significant at the 0.05 level, or better.

This model was estimated using OLS with the expectation that β_{61} would remain significant after adding the new variables. Also, the estimated signs of the level of development and its interaction with the diversity of the economic structure should both be negative, indicating that their influence tends to decrease inequality. The short-term boost variable, however, should have an opposite, positive sign. Table 3.3 and Figure 3.2 present the regression results which fit the theoretical expectations rather well.

The empirical evaluation of the model meets with fairly strong "success": the expected sign of each individual relationship is in the predicted direction, the strength of each specified relationship is relatively robust, the overall fit of the entire equation is high, each estimated coefficient is statistically different from chance, and the F-test for the entire equation is itself statistically significant. It must be noted, however, that the problems discussed in the analysis of the individual effect of the level of development upon inequality have not disappeared and must be kept in mind in discussing the results. Additionally, the problem of multicollinearity has been introduced since the interaction term

FIGURE 3.2. Schematic Representation of the Linkages Between the Development Process and Inequality[a]

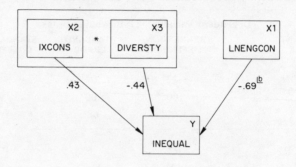

Equation (3.6) $Y = -.69(X1) + .43(X2) - .44(X2 \cdot X3)$

$\overline{R2^c} = .60 \qquad F = 22.47 \qquad p = .001$

---

a. Where: INEQUAL   (Y) = Composite inequality index
            LNENGCON (X1) = Natural logarithm of energy consumption per capita
            IXCONS   (X2) = Index of construction activity
            DIVERSTY (X3) = Index of the diversity of the economic infrastructure
   These variables and their components are explained in greater detail in Appendix B wherein reference is
   made to their introduction into the text.
b. Standardized regression coefficients are reported. For more complete information on estimation, see
   Table 3.3. All estimates are statistically significant at the 0.05 level or better.
c. Corrected coefficient of determination is equivalent to the percent of variance in the dependent variable
   which is explained by the independent variables.
* This symbol represents multiplicative interaction.

$(X2 \cdot X3)$ is analytically composed using one of the other "independent" variables, X2. Empirically, the relationship between these two "independent" variables is strong (r = .85) and they share over sixty percent covariation. Kmenta (1971) summarizes some loose tests of the harmfulness of multicollinearity thus: (1) the difference between the total $\overline{R2}$ and the highest individual $\overline{R2}$ is small, (2) the level of the overall F statistic is significant while at the same time no individual t-test of the significance of individual coefficients is itself significant. Even if any of these "tests" points to harmful collinearity, very little can be done to alleviate the problem save increasing the stock of available information—by adding cases and/or variables. While none of the tests suggested by Kmenta indicates severe multicollinearity, it still seems clear that there is enough to cause some problems in the consistency of the estimates. However, even severe multicollinearity does not necessarily invalidate the test of the model; rather, it weakens the power of the test itself. In any case, in keeping with the overall philosophy which seeks to interpret the residuals theoretically, the "solution" of adding more information is exactly what is to be accomplished in the subsequent modules.

3.4 SUMMARY

This chapter has concerned itself with one overriding task: to construct and evaluate a model that relates the internal aspects of economic development to the distribution of societal equality in a polity. Three links between development variables were established on the basis of theoretical arguments developed here and elsewhere. Of these, the strongest link is between the level of development and inequality. Both the theoretical and empirical evidence strongly suggest that high levels of equality are associated with high levels of development. The converse also seems well informed, as there is a virtual myriad of polities with high inequality and low development. On the surface this contradicts the arguments of many, though not all, neo-Marxists who argue that development decreases equality.

However, if the second-order effects of growth are considered, it may be expected that rapid growth will have a negative effect on the equality of the social and economic distribution of values. Again, considerable evidence was found to support this theoretical position. Finally, it was argued that the impact of growth upon equality was mediated by the interaction of growth and the diversity of the economic structure. That is, economic systems which do not concentrate growth into single sectors tend to spread the growth throughout the entire system in such a way as to bring about decreasing levels of inequality. This argument was also empirically evaluated and strong support for it was found.

Based upon theoretical and empirical evidence, it has been argued that there is a negative, logarithmic relationship between economic development and inequality in modern political systems. The effects of rapid economic growth and the diversity of the economic structure have also been explored. The empirical support presented in this chapter for the first of these linkages, that between development and inequality, largely replicates the evidence offered by Jackman, though it was based upon a more recent and more exhaustive sample of polities, as well as on an "independent" set of observations.

Another competing explanation may be offered which addresses this argument, and which is specifically concerned with the configuration of the scattergram presented in Figure 3.1, and the statistical findings as reported in Tables 3.1 and 3.2.

It may be that, rather than a single logarithmic model, two distinct processes govern the relationship between development and inequality. It must be remembered that the static analysis undertaken here, and in the work of Jackman, is offered as an approximation of the underlying longitudinal process. Granting that inference for the moment, suppose that below a certain threshold of development, roughly corresponding to the oft-invoked division of the world into First and Second, as opposed to Third and Fourth Worlds, a strong, linear, negative relationship existed. For the more developed nations above that threshold, however, a different, more moderate linkage held between these two phenomena.

Such an explanatory scheme is not much different in form from the logarithmic specification unless one considers the inferred, longitudinal movement toward higher levels of development. In the curvilinear form, as nations develop, they receive decreasing returns to the level of equality as the logarithmic curve bends sharply and begins to level off. However, theoretically it is possible, other things being equal, for a polity to traverse the entire range of both variables. In the process version, it may be that the more moderate linear relationship will never be appropriate for those polities for which the strong linkage is applicable. Thus, it may be that in a longitudinal, historical sense, nations may be constrained from achieving high levels of development and equality.

This is precisely the type of argument being offered by many scholars under the rubric of *dependencia* or dependency theory. Dos Santos (1970), Cardoso (1973), Jaguaribe (1974), and Cardoso and Faletto (1977) are prominent Latin American scholars of this tradition. Basically, these arguments suggest that because of the invidious nature of the international division of labor, there is associated, dependent—and even distorted—development in those nations less centrally integrated into the global economic system. This nationalistic, structuralist viewpoint has broadened beyond its Latin beginnings to the idea that it is structurally difficult or impossible for the current international economic and political configuration to allow nondistorted, nondependent development in currently disadvantaged nations.[4] This *dependencia* idea is very similar to the one extant in American politics that institutional racism, whether purposive or not, underlies the relative position of blacks and whites.

[80]

It is interesting that those Latin American countries which gave rise to the initial dependency ideas are spread along the low-to-medium development and high inequality regions which might be captured by the steep curve in a two-process explanation. However, none have made the transition to the higher levels of development and equality which would be captured by the moderate curve hypothesized by the second process. These dependency ideas cannot easily be rejected. Neither can they, in this work, be explored much further, since longitudinal evidence will clearly be required.

The above research does not resolve many of the differences between Marxist and classical interpretations of the phenomenon of economic growth and its implications and consequences. It does, however, provide a synthesis of the elements of several important lines of economic thought and scholarship. This synthesis is found to have considerable merit when considered both theoretically and empirically. Many factors are still omitted, and several of these will be explored in subsequent chapters. What has been accomplished in addition to the synthesis is the construction of a somewhat validated—though simplified—model which is based upon internal economic considerations. This nexus can serve as the starting point for the incorporation of other economic and political factors both international and subnational which are to be considered in the remainder of this work. Three broad categories of variables remain to be included: (1) the internal political, organizational, and historical; (2) the international and transnational economic; and (3) the international and transnational political.

In addition to the differences between Jackman (1975) and the present study already discussed, one remaining point requires emphasis. The basic driving variable in the model thus far is the level of development. It is argued that the basic relationship between development and inequality is negative and curvilinear. The *raison d'etre* for introducing the curvilinear aspect of this relationship is based upon the incomplete nature of the model. Kuznets and many followers have argued that at the upper end of the development process political factors come into play which invoke a threshold.[5] Thus, the curvilinearity is really a surrogate for these other factors. Jackman's analysis, for example, adopts the curvilinear relationship and attempts to build in some of the other factors suggested by Kuznets. However, in attempting to model these other factors, he does not attempt to remove the curvilinearity that serves as their surrogate in the more simplified model. This study will attempt to remove that surrogate by specifically modeling that which it attempts to represent.

N O T E S

1. The use of terms like development, development process, developed nations, underdeveloped, and undeveloped is somewhat misleading without an explicit definition of what is meant by them. Their usage here is not intended to convey any historical necessity, linear progression, or cultural imperialism. Moul (1974) has expounded upon the inadequacies of many conceptualizations prevalent in many current works. One prominent study of political development is Jaguaribe (1973).

   By "development" here is meant the idea of industrialization and diversification of an economic system. A highly developed economy is one which is relatively stable and strong, and accordingly has the ability to provide a high level of economic product. Thus, developed societies need not necessarily be highly industrialized, though usually they are. Rather than use the most common production oriented measure of development, Gross National Product, an operational indicator is utilized which aims at measuring the *per capita* consumption of energy: consumption of metric tons of coal equivalents *per* head (ENGCON).

2. See Kmenta (1971:197-246) or Hilton (1976:43-46) for a more formal treatment of these assumptions. Some familiarity with econometrics will be assumed throughout many of the following discussions.

3. This does not affect the properties of the estimates unless the stochastic variable and the error term are either serially or cross-sectionally correlated. In these cases the estimates may not have any or all of the desired characteristics. See Kmenta (1971:298-300).

4. Caporaso (1978) has edited a special edition of *International Organization* entitled *Dependence and Dependency in the Global System* which reviews many of these *dependencia* ideas. Other important, broad-gauge work in this area includes: Frank (1969), Furtado (1970), Galtung (1971), Bonilla and Girling (1973), Amin (1973), Chilcote (1974), Wallerstein (1974), and Senghaas (1975).

5. See Kuznets' earlier quote on page 56 of this chapter.

R E F E R E N C E S

Adelman, I. and C. Morris (1967). Society, Politics, and Economic Development: A Quantitative Approach. Baltimore, Md.: Johns Hopkins Press.

Adelman, I. and C. Morris (1973). Economic Growth and Social Equity in Developing Countries. Stanford: Stanford University Press.

Amin, S. (1973). Accumulation on a World Scale: A Critique of the Theory of Underdevelopment. New York: Monthly Review Press.

Anscombe, F. (1973). "Graphs in Statistical Analysis." American Statistician, Vol. 27, pp 17-21.

Baran, P. (1958). "On the Political Economy of Backwardness." in A. Agarwala and S. Singh, (eds.) The Economics of Underdevelopment. New York: Oxford University Press.

Bonilla, F. and R. Girling, editors (1973). Structures of Dependence. Stanford, California: Institute of Political Studies.

Caporaso, J., (editor, 1978). Dependence and Dependency in the Global System. International Organization, Vol. 32, No. 1, entire.

Cardoso, F. H. (1973). "Imperialism and Dependency in Latin America." Pp 7-16 in Bonilla and Girling (1973).

Cardoso, F. H. and E. Faletto (1977). Dependency and Development in Latin America. Berkeley, California: University of California Press.

Chenery, H. and L. Taylor (1968). "Development Patterns: Among Countries and Over Time." The Review of Economics and Statistics, Vol. 50, No. 4, pp 391-416.

Chenery, H., S. Ahluwalia, C. L. G. Bell, J. H. Duloy, and R. Jolly (1974). Redistribution with Growth. New York: Oxford University Press.

Chenery, H., M. Syrquin, with H. Elkington (1975). Patterns of Development, 1950-1970. New York: Oxford University Press.

Chilcote, R. H. (1974). "Dependency: A Critical Synthesis of the Literature." Latin American Perspective, Vol. 1, No. 1, pp 4-29.

Cutright, P. (1967). "Inequality: A Cross-National Analysis." American Sociological Review, Vol. 32, pp 562-578.

Dos Santos, T. (1970). "The Structure of Dependence." American Economic Review, Vol. 60, No. 2, pp 231-236.

Frank, A. G. (1969). Latin America: Underdevelopment or Revolution. New York: Monthly Review Press.

Furtado, C. (1971). Development and Underdevelopment: A Structural View of the Problems of Developed and Underdeveloped Countries. Berkeley, California: University of California Press.

Galtung, J. (1971). "A Structural Theory of Imperialism." Journal of Peace Research, Vol. 3, No. 2, pp 81-119.

Hilton, G. (1976). Intermediate Politometrics. New York: Columbia University Press.

Herfindal, O. C. (1950). "Concentration in the Steel Industry." Unpublished Ph.D. Dissertation, Columbia University.

Jackman, R. W. (1975). Politics and Social Equality. New York: John Wiley.

Jaguaribe, H. (1973). Political Development: A General Theory and a Latin American Case Study. New York: Harper and Row.

Jain, S. (1975). Distribution of Income: A Compilation of Data. Washington, D.C.: The World Bank.

Kmenta, J. (1971). Elements of Econometrics. New York: The Macmillan Company.

Kravis, I. (1960). "International Differences in the Distribution of Income." Review of Economics and Statistics, Vol. 42, pp 408-416.

Kuznets, S. (1955). "Economic Growth and Income Inequality." American Economic Review, Vol. 45, pp 1-28.

Kuznets, S. (1963). "Quantitative Aspects of the Economic Growth of Nations, VIII: The Distribution of Income by Size." Economic Development and Cultural Change, Vol. 11, Part 2 (entire).

Lenski, G. (1966). Power and Privilege: A Theory of Social Stratification. New York: McGraw Hill.

Morgan, J. and R. Sondquist (1967). The Automatic Interaction Detector. Ann Arbor: University of Michigan Press.

Moul, W. B. (1974). "On Getting Nothing for Something: A Note on Causal Models of Political Development." Comparative Political Studies, Vol. 7, No. 2, pp 139-164.

Myrdal, G. (1953). The Political Element in the Development of Economic Theory. London: Routledge and Kegan Paul Ltd.

Myrdal, G. (1973). Against the Stream: Critical Essays on Economics. New York: Pantheon Books.

Olson, M. (1963). "Rapid Growth as a Destabilizing Force." Journal of Economic History, Vol. 23, pp 529-552.

Ranis, G. (1975). "Equity and Growth." Journal of Conflict Resolution, Vol. 19, No. 3, pp 558-568.

Ray, J. L. and J. D. Singer (1973). "Measuring the Concentration of Power in the International System." Sociological Methods and Research, Vol. I, No. 4, pp 403-437.

Senghaas, D. (1975). "Multinational Corporations and the Third World: On the Problem of the Further Integration of Peripheries into the Given Structure of the International Economic System." Journal of Peace Research, Vol. 12, No. 4, pp 257-274.

Tufte, E., editor (1970). The Quantitative Analysis of Social Problems. Reading, Mass.: Addison-Wesley.

Tufte, E. (1974). Data Analysis for Politics and Policy. Englewood Cliffs, New Jersey: Prentice-Hall.

United Nations (1974). Yearbook of Construction Statistics 1962-1972. Geneva: The United Nations.

Wallerstein, I. (1974). The Modern World System. New York: Academic Press.

The Impact of Political and Public Policy upon Inequalities in Contemporary Polities

4

4.1 INTRODUCTION

The primary goal of this chapter is to supplement theoretically and empirically the economic arguments made in the previous chapter concerning the internal determinants of inequality in the distribution of material and social goods in the contemporary polity. These domestically oriented arguments were primarily economic in nature, exploring the relationships among the level of economic development, the growth of that development, the diversity of the economic infrastructure, and the distribution of welfare. Unfortunately, the adoption of these economic ideas by other social scientists more directly concerned with the sociological and political aspects of distribution has not provided a great deal of amplification beyond the economic bases originally laid by the economists.

Accordingly, despite the overt reliance upon economic theory, one of the dominant components of these theories has been a strong and implicit dependence upon political factors to embellish and flesh out the line of argument posed in the overall explanatory frameworks. Most economists, however, have shown little interest in explicitly specifying these assumptions about the relationship between political and economic phenomena that proved so crucial to their ideas about development and equality. Furthermore, many empirical economists are fundamentally opposed to the possibility of quantifying data which are not easily expressed in monetary terms. This parochialism has been duly noted by scholars, including some economists, and attempts have been made to include political phenomena in their causal schema either as causes or effects, or both. The work of Adelman and Morris (1973) among others has been exemplary in this respect.

Building upon prior theoretical and empirical work in economics, notably that of Kuznets (1955, 1963), a specification of some of the political assumptions is required for a fuller explanation of the relationships among the internal characteristics of a polity which precondition its distributional patterns. Implicit in this incorporation of political factors into the overall model of distribution is the reexamination of the economic factors with which the exploration was begun.

Apart from the need to be less exclusive about the causes of inequality that are themselves resident within the polity, other reasons give rise to the need to include elements which are explicitly political. The most general of these is based upon the comprehensiveness of the model. It is neither intuitively obvious nor deductively clear why economic wealth alone should promote equality. Yet, the empirical association between these two phenomena is a strong one. The previous chapter provided some theory and data to suggest part of the mechanics which translate that economic wealth into different patterns of equality. However, that specification leaves two crucial areas unattended: (1) mass participation and political mobilization and (2) policy effort. Moreover, assumptions about these two concepts are incorporated into the crux of the economic argument. First of all, it is argued here that policies formulated to promote the linkage between wealth and equality provide one necessary component of the overall picture. Historically, this has been the case, inasmuch as few polities endowed with a high degree of wealth and exhibiting a minimal policy effort also have witnessed minimal levels of inequality. Second, it is exceedingly unlikely that such policies, whether successful or unsuccessful, will arise in a vacuum. On the contrary, they will tend to arise in situations in which decision-making elites perceive either the benefits of such policies or the costs of their absence. Such awareness is often stimulated by mass participation and demand; other times it is brought forth by ideological commitment. Both aspects are important, for each represents two somewhat different political movements. As conceptualized here, each represents a particular manifestation of political mobilization. In these terms, the extent of demands placed upon the bureaucracies of the polity for increased equality are also a necessary part of the search for an explanation of inequality based upon factors largely internal to the nation state. Conversely, it seems plausible that without a fairly high level of wealth to (re)distribute, policy effort in this area, when stimulated by indigenous demands, is unlikely to have much impact upon the actual distribution of welfare.

These two influences, the scope and extent of demands for increased sharing of the economic and social product of a polity and the success and experience of the bureaucracy in fulfilling those demands, represent the bulk of the implicit political argument made by economists such as Kuznets as to the reason for the tapering off of the effect of economic development on decreased inequality. More importantly, these political factors must be blended into the body of the argument by which economic development is posited to bring about decreased levels of inequality. Thus, these political elements may be conjoined with the economic arguments in order to effect a more precise statement of the theoretical perspective and to formulate a more appropriate examination of empirical evidence which can be brought to bear upon these ideas.

This chapter utilizes the concepts of policy effort and political mobilization in order to uncover part of the political constituent hidden in the economic formulation, as presented above. Without both demands for increased participation in the sharing of material product as well as concerted policy efforts aimed at fulfilling those demands, the impact of higher levels of development on inequality is unlikely to be large. In fact, these aspects represent what is often referred to as the social and political side of economic development.

Moreover, is important to consider these two political phenomena precisely for the policy content which they add. They represent relevant variables which can be manipulated to an extent by planners and bureaucrats within the modern polity. In fact, these variables, among others, have provided much of the nexus of the social "experiments" attempted by communist and socialist forms of societal and market organization. Not only do these two simple ideas provide a linkage to the bulk of modern democratic theory, but they also suggest policy fulcrums for adapting the outcomes of distributional policies of all types of political systems to the demands generated within those polities.

4.2 A Policy Perspective on Development and Equality

Development economics has been much studied from a policy perspective. Much of the wisdom, such as it is, of that subdiscipline is based upon its efforts to suggest what types of economic policies would

[87]

best foster increased economic productivity. Pursuit of economic development by active rather than passive means has characterized the decision-making bodies of most post-World War II governmental organizations, ranging from the local to the international level. The scope of this activity, which might be called development policy planning, includes the preparation of budgets as well as the design of specific programs aimed at restricting or enhancing the reactivity of bread prices, say, to projected wheat yields. Such policies may be designed in response to actual, current situations and conditions, or in response to forecasts of future possibilities. Further, policies may be either preventative or prosthetic. In the final analysis, policies are adjudged to be either successful or unsuccessful.

The basic paradigm of modern development economics is based upon the work of Marshall (1920, 1952). A fundamental premise of this paradigm is its conception of economic activity as a continuous process governed by equilibrium processes. Thus, processes "correct" themselves for any slight aberrations from the theoretical predictions that may crop up. Furthermore, this neoclassical framework places great importance upon the somewhat optimistic notion that surplus production in one realm of an economy, be it geographical, organizational, or sectoral, eventually will tend to spread to all other realms of the economic structure; therefore, the benefits will "trickle down" through the rest of the economy until all of it is permeated with the rewards of growth and increased productivity. In this way, economic development, in the form of surplus productivity, cannot fail to serve the whole of the economic structure as well as all of its components.

Based upon this view, one might argue, policies should be sought that will accelerate this process of growth, since it so obviously will benefit all members of the society in the long run. This argument is not a fictitious one, and much of the policy planning in the post-War era has been concerned with precisely this activity. A long list of archetypical policy arenas will not necessarily strengthen this argument, but if offered they might include the analysis of import substitution, production functions and decomposition, behavior of the firm and the regulations governing it, policies to enhance technological change as well as its spread, trade barriers and customs unions, and any number of familiar areas of economic planning.

The fact that much of development planning has also centered on how to maximize manpower utilization, control unemployment in various isolated sectors, as well as the economy in general, and eliminate inequality itself suggests, if nothing else, that the neoclassical account is problematic at least in its application, if not in its optimism. Presumably, economic planning under the neoclassical scheme should not include more than momentary excursions into these "problem areas" which have so often plagued modern and modernizing societies.

Viewed most broadly, the record of development has nonetheless been very strong. A recent survey (Yotopoulos and Nugent, 1976:5) notes that the average growth in Gross Domestic Product (GDP) has increased at a rate of approximately five percent in the 1950-1969 period for both the developed and the less-developed nations. However, unemployment has been a problem of enormous magnitude in the less developed nations, as has been the rapid—if not Malthusian—growth of population. Both these facts have several important implications: (1) an increased level of inequality in the less developed nations, and (2) failure of the "natural" adaptive mechanisms of the neoclassical account to effect adjustments toward the equilibrium condition prescribed by it. Paraphrasing Yotopoulos and Nugent (1976:238), it seems obvious that one of the major problems in contemporary nations is that the institutions which promote economic growth themselves are not indifferent to the distribution of economic and social product. These observations, in part, have provided much fuel for the more recent Marxist arguments which present emphatic criticism of the neoclassical approach.

Furthermore, the social fabric, when viewed more comprehensively in terms of its political, sociocultural, and historical aspects, is apparently governed by a somewhat different, or at least more inclusive, set of equilibrium mechanisms than the purely economic ones suggested by Marshallian theory. The upshot of this is that policy need concern itself with many of the shortcomings, or blind spots, of development economics if it is to succeed in smoothing over the "blemishes" which recent history has so persistently uncovered. Both sides of the coin, the neoclassical and the Marxist, then, show the same suggestion: policy is important in translating economic product into economic and social benefit.

Thus, for both theoretical and empirical reasons, it seems clear that the impact of public policy is a relevant variable of potential importance in the search for the causal mechanisms that regulate the distribution of economic and social product in the contemporary political system. It is argued here that in polities showing large amounts of inequality, public policy measures alone will necessarily be insufficient to effect drastic redistributions of economic and social product which will be vastly more egalitarian. It may well be that policy efforts will be ineffectual even in polities which have the requisite economic base. More specifically, while in general, policy effort aimed at redistribution, when coupled with a sufficient level of (re)distributable product, will tend to reduce inequality, in specific cases certain types of policy efforts will be efficient to a lesser or greater extent.

In light of the foregoing, it seems altogether likely that public policy efforts not only supplement the causal linkage between development and equality but also may mediate it. Public policy is one of the most important mechanisms likely to promote the translation of economic product into more egalitarian distributions of that product. It is this formulation which is herein explored. This view is consonant with much of what has been written in the field of developmental economics, and it is consistent with many of the divergent attempts to correct not only the flaws in Marshallian theory, but also those evident in the distribution of social and economic product in developed and developing nations.

The inclusion of this policy aspect is sought on the one hand to promote the inclusiveness and completeness of the overall model. Additionally, the inclusion of policy variables should provide a possible common ground of interaction between theories which promote the Marshallian view of economic development and distribution and those more radical-structuralist theories, largely Marxist, which argue that economic growth and development are not necessarily beneficial to the social structure as a whole, inasmuch as they are frequently accompanied by increasing levels of inequality. Thus, once policy variables indicative of both behavioral and structural factors operating within the social structure of the polity are taken into account, the differences between these two accounts is somewhat lessened.

It should be pointed out that Marxist ideology and theory are not monolithic in regard to these ideas. Among the several variants which might usefully be differentiated are nineteenth century European Marxism, contemporary European socialism, and Third World Marxist ideology. This study does justice to none of these arguments. Rather, it presents a broad-gauge general perspective aimed only at highlighting the grossest distinctions between (neo)-Ricardian and (neo)-Marxist theoretical orientation.

Although the empirical findings of the previous chapter indicate much more surface congruence with the Marshallian account of economic development and equality, many studies, as has been pointed out, have found contrary results. As yet, however, there is no definitive set of answers to the theoretical questions posed by these two broad sets of theory. On the whole, the theoretical arguments and the bulk of the empirical evidence seem to fall on the side of the neoclassical account. However, this statement must be interpreted in an extremely guarded fashion, since each account can find serious theoretical and empirical criticism of the others. Furthermore, these two accounts focus upon somewhat different aspects of the entire picture—the Marshallian account being largely economic, and the Marxist account, in its most recent forms, being primarily sociological. This latter point also suggests the utility of the more inclusive models, which encompass political elements, and which perhaps can serve to integrate the wisdoms of each intellectual and policy tradition.

A comparative analysis of the multitude of policy attempts to influence the distribution of material and social product would require a much expanded format. Broadly, one can easily identify various categories of policy which are specific enough to retain their meaningfulness as manipulable variables while at the same time general enough to facilitate comparison and permit inclusion. Chenery et al. (1974) have suggested several. The scope of this list includes social as well as economic, domestic as well as international, and public as well as private policy measures: (1) taxation policy, (2) land reform, (3) nationalization of foreign and/or domestic enterprises, (4) basic educational programs as well as highly specialized eductional programs of technical and organizational nature, (5) provision of public goods (social welfare) through governmental and nongovernmental means, (6) consumption transfers, and (7 and 8) agricultural and industrial policies. Not all of these policies are attempted by every polity seeking to redistribute social product, though frequently many are utilized. Many are inappropriate in some situations while potentially powerful in others. The appropriateness and the effectiveness of such policies are related but certainly not isomorphic.

Each of the above policy areas has been studied in its own right. However, three of these—land reform, education, and social welfare programs—have received the most persistent and intense attention of scholars and policy planners alike. Of these three only the latter two, education and social welfare, will receive attention here. There are several reasons for this, aside from the need for parsimony. Empirical studies have focused on these two as exhibiting the most consistently beneficial effects upon the distribution of social product. That is not to say that there is unanimity of thought on this topic: far from it. Nonetheless, if there is any consensus about which policies are most likely to have any effect upon equality, it is on these two. The area of land reform has also been fairly productive in terms of what various advantages and disadvantages it may pose for equality, but it is more strictly applicable to polities which are highly agricultural in their organization, rather than to the more expansive set of polities under investigation here. Educational policies and social welfare programs, on the other hand, present a more broadly applicable set of policy tools. Furthermore, they have been pushed for more intensively by localized political movements such as political parties and labor organizations. As such, they more properly embody the "political" component being investigated here. These two areas, then, are potentially applicable and have been attempted in virtually every type of polity—from the poorest to the richest, from the most egalitarian to the least.

4.3 SOCIAL WELFARE POLICIES

At the most basic level, social welfare policy is defined as the attempt by governmental or nongovernmental organizations seeking either (1) expansion of previously private goods into the public sector, or (2) increases in the scope and the degree of public goods available to the citizenry of a polity. Operationally, this study largely restricts its focus to welfare policy attempted by governmental organizations which are themselves resident within the polity. The literature on public goods is vast and requires no summary at this juncture; the meaning and intention of the term are well established (Olson, 1965; Buchanan, 1968).

Empirically, the search for the impact of social welfare policy on the distribution of material and social product has centered upon programs aimed at providing social insurance to the populace, usually defined in terms of the working members of the potential labor force. The general idea has been that should something happen to a member of the labor force—such as aging, retirement, disability, or unemployment—the

[92]

social insurance program would be able to provide enough institutional and monetary support to sustain such affected individuals at least at minimal levels.

The history of social insurance programs is a long one, and more recently they have included a wide range of services for all members of the polity regardless of their current situation. Irrespective of their extensiveness, all such programs are redistributive in the sense that they affect the transfers of services and income across a wide range of "boundaries" separating different groups of people. Old-age programs attempt to redistribute wages and services throughout the life cycle by providing these goods to members of society long after they have left the productive labor force. Unemployment insurance, another common form of social insurance, also is redistributive with regard to those members of society who are temporarily outside the active labor force, since they receive products and services generated by those still active.

The pioneering work of Phillips Cutright (1965, 1967) has focused on this social insurance thrust from an operational perspective, and many have built upon his initial work in investigating the linkages between social welfare policy and inequality from a more theoretical framework. His initial contribution was the discovery and presentation of cross-national data on social security programs, collected by the U.S. Social Security Administration. While working for that agency, Cutright uncovered this cross-national material and began its systematic analysis. A major kingpin in his contribution was the construction of an index based upon data about different types of social insurance programs. That index, the social insurance program experience index—later accepted in its acronym form by many scholars (SIPE), basically measured the number of years of experience a country had with various social insurance programs. He analyzed the five categories of insurance definitionally imposed by the Social Security Agency (SSA): work-injury programs, illness programs, old-age programs, family allowance programs, and unemployment insurance.

Utilizing scalogram analysis, Cutright found that these five "items" formed a nearly perfect Guttman-scale (with reproducibility greater than 0.96). This means that the five types of program are ordinally ranked, so that a country with no experience with any of these programs would be given the lowest score, while a country with all five of the programs would be given the highest Guttman-scale score. Fur-

[93]

thermore, what this ordering, which as presented above was taken from Cutright's original analysis, implies is that work-injury programs are the most likely to occur and therefore, in terms of the scale, least difficult to achieve, while the unemployment programs are the most difficult to achieve; and that a society with unemployment insurance is almost certain to have each of the other programs as well. Based upon this Guttman scalogram analysis, Cutright's index was calculated as the sum of the number of years of experience—defined in terms of existence of the program—between 1934 and 1960 which a polity had with each of the five programs. Thus, the maximum score was twenty-seven (the number of years) times five (the number of programs). It was this index which served as Cutright's SIPE index.

Cutright used this measure as a dependent as well as independent variable in several different studies. On the one hand, he was interested in examining the covariation between an index of political representativeness, and on the other, he was interested in the relationship between inequality and a nation's experience with social security programs.

Two camps characterize the empirical literature that was spurred by Cutright's initial test of Lenski's model of the intervening impact public policy exerts on the relationship between economic development and inequality. One argues that the effects of policy are negligible in comparison with the greater impact of economic variables. The other position emphasizes the individual importance of "democratic" performance. This study will not explicitly limit itself to examining the effects of democratic performance or policy; rather, the basic hypothesis that policy is an important intervening variable will be examined in polities of all types of political and social organization. This is not to dismiss the actual impact of empirical work.

Harold Wilensky (1975) is one of the few scholars to attempt rigorous comparisons of equality across East and West. Like so many researchers, he has focused upon expenditures of government agencies in providing for social insurance. Additionally, more work has been done by Echols (1975) in comparing regional inequality in a few selected communist and capitalist systems. Recent summary and empirical examination of this question in a modern democratic theory framework is given in Jackman (1975). While his conceptualization is much different than that presented here, and is also limited to a moderate sample (N = 60) of noncommunist countries, Jackman basically finds that

SIPE is an intervening variable between economic activity and distributional patterns in 1960 polities. This finding supports the basic argument as pursued here.

The major differences between the inequality index utilized in Jackman's work (the Schutz coefficient) and that used here have been previously discussed. Furthermore, the differences in the conceptualization of the economic aspects of development and equality were also made clear. Jackman's use of the SIPE index is also rejected in this study. First of all, one major objection to the SIPE index may be lodged purely on the basis that it does not make use of the powerful information generated by Cutrights' own original analysis. Since an ordering of program types was produced by the scalogram analysis, at a minimum it should have served as a weight for the eventual calculation of the SIPE index. The most likely candidate, of course, would have been the Guttman scale scores. Moreover, the SIPE index only makes use of one aspect of information about the past experience of a nation state with a program of social insurance—the length of experience. It contains no information about the success of such a program, how extensively it is used or modified, the source of funds to operate such programs, or the scope of coverage. Information of this sort was not available to Cutright; thus, SIPE was (and is) a crude indicator of historical experience.

Presently, a much wider range of data on the social insurance of virtually every contemporary polity is being collected by the SSA. Of the five types of programs originally defined by the SSA, relatively complete and current information is available on three: (1) unemployment programs, (2) old-age coverage, and (3) workman's compensation. Furthermore, in addition to being more up-to-date (collected in 1973), data are available on the extent of coverage in each of these three plans with respect to what percentage of the labor force is covered by them, the sources of funding for such plans—ranging from funds provided by the worker only to plans which are entirely sponsored by the government, the extent of benefits in terms of the percentage of earnings provided by them, as well as the year of origin and the date of the most recent modification. Since they should reflect a much more precise picture of policy effort in these areas, these five variables have been coded by the author for each of the three types of social insurance areas. The operational codings are given in Table 4.1.

Based upon these data for 120 contemporary polities, a factor

TABLE 4.1. *Operational Definitions of Unemployment, Work-Injury, and Old-Age Compensation Programs in Contemporary Polities**

VARIABLES	DEFINITIONS
Year of origin	Number of years in which the program was operative, (Scored negatively)
Year of most recent modification	Number of years since the last major revision of the program. (Current Base = 1972).
Scope of coverage	All employees = 2
	Some employees = 1
	No employees = 0
Source of funds	Primarily governmental = 5
	Governmental and industrial = 4
	Governmental, industrial and individual contributions = 3
	Primarily industrial = 2
	Individual contributions only = 1
	No program = 0
Benefits as percent of weekly earnings	100% − 80 = 5
	79 − 60 = 4
	59 − 40 = 3
	39 − 20 = 2
	19 − 0% = 0

*All data were coded by the author from information provided in *Social Security Programs Throughout the World, 1973*, Research Report #44, The Social Security Administration, Washington, D.C.

analysis was performed in order to seek an index which could be used to reflect a more complete picture of a polity's policy effort in the social insurance area. The results of the analysis are presented in Table 4.2. The factor structure is quite clear and interpretable. Three factors emerge, each of which corresponds to the types of programs which were originally codified. The uniqueness of each program, in terms of the factor structure, suggests that there are varying degrees of social insurance programs in contemporary polities and that the existence of any one type of program does not imply the existence of other programs.

In each factor, the variables reflecting the age of the program and the recentness of its major modifications have the highest loadings. It should be noted that information on the year of origin of unemployment and work-injury programs was available for only thirty seven polities; accordingly, these variables were not included in the analysis. However, the age variables are correlated greater than 0.9 with their corresponding modification variables. This correlation, based upon only 37 cases, suggests (1) that the exclusion of the age variable will presumably not greatly affect the factor structure, and (2) that polities with long historical experience with social insurance programs are also likely to have made major modifications in them recently.

Keeping in mind Cutright's original finding, that unemployment programs are the most difficult to achieve and the least likely to occur, the factor score representing unemployment variables (labeled "UNEMPL") was chosen as an operationalization of the variable con-

TABLE 4.2. *Factor Analysis of Social Security Programs* *

VARIABLE	Factor		
	OLD AGE	UNEMPLOYMENT	INJURY
AGEYMOD	96		
AGECOV	80		
AGEFUND	76		
AGEBENE	72		
UNYRMOD		93	
UNCOV		93	
UNFUND		92	
UNBENE		92	
WKYRMOD			74
WKCOV			64
WKFUND			55
WKBENE			65
Pct. Variance	40	33	17

* Varimax rotated factor matrix, orthogonal rotation, and Kaiser normalization. All values except the eigenvalues have been multiplied by 100 in order to eliminate the decimals. Only loadings greater than 50 have been presented.

[97]

cerned with policy effort in social insurance programs. This index combines information on the year of the last major modification, the scope of coverage, the source of funds, and the extent of benefits of unemployment insurance programs in 120 contemporary nations. A polity receiving a high score on this index is one with a long history of experience in administering such programs, one that has sought to make major modifications, typically extensions, in these programs in recent years, has a high degree of governmental involvement in providing funds to sustain such programs, has extensive rather than exclusive rules of eligibility for the benefits of such programs, and has a high level of benefits which are provided through such programs.

Thus, in addition to providing a larger, more contemporary set of data, this index is itself more extensive in the aspects of policy effort it measures than was the earlier SIPE index. This new index (UNEM-FAC) will be used to examine the proposition that policy variables mediate the effects of development and growth.

Another social welfare policy which has played an important role in empirical investigations into the question of inequality has been the effect of education. Most of this inquiry has been directed to the possibility that education increases the skills, and therefore the potential participation, of citizens in a modernizing society. However, the place of education in postindustrial societies is also of great importance. The answers as to whether education can serve to promote equality must be given, so far, in somewhat guarded terms. Nonetheless, the studies of education's relation to the political and economic aspects of development have been abundant, and for the most part relatively sophisticated. A survey of the literature will not be conducted here, but the interested reader might start with the works of Jencks and associates (1972) from an American perspective, and the works of Chiswick (1974) for the most comprehensive study in a cross-national and historical perspective. Raymond Boudon's (1974) brilliant analysis of education and social mobility is also very important.

Chiswick, among others, has conceptualized the contribution of education to development and possibly equality in terms of human capital. The basic finding of his study is that the distribution of income is often related to the investments a society makes in human capital, education being one of the most important of these investments. From a policy perspective, one might add that this aspect of human capital lies largely within the realm of governmental control. In addition to the findings of Chiswick, Chenery and associates (1975) have also shown that education exerts a positive influence on the distribution of income. They utilized the primary and secondary school enrollment rates to estimate the impact of educational policy on equality. Their finding was that while both variables do not at the same time produce significant results, the inclusion of either one in the equality equation is sufficient for the production of a significant coefficient. Interestingly, they also found that the primary school enrollment is "more significant in explaining S3 [the income share of the bottom 40 percent of the population], while the secondary school enrollment rate is more significant in explaining S2 [the share of income held by the middle 40 percent of the population]."

Educational policy, with social welfare policy as derived above, will be used as an indicator of attempts by the polity to effect redistribution of wealth within the social structure. Several obvious operational indicators exist for the measurement of such a variable: percentage of governmental budget devoted to education, percentage of the population enrolled in school, the literacy rate, the number of schools, *et cetera*.

However, sufficient data are at present relatively unavailable on such measures for the large sample of contemporary polities in the present study. The operational indicator that was chosen—the number of universities or colleges present in any given polity—was selected for two reasons: (1) the availability of such data for each of the 120 polities, and (2) its conceptual correspondence to the thrust of the theoretical and empirical arguments which suggested the importance of education.

This measure is, however, recognizably biased toward educational policies which on the whole are more readily available to the upper income strata (of both individuals and nations) than to the lower. It should also be recognized that the number of universities is more indicative of the quantity of high-level and generally technical education than it is of widespread, mass-oriented educational policies which aim at achieving literacy and involvement. For example, the number of universities is found to be highly related to the number of scholars a nation sends abroad ($r = 0.70$) and to the number of medical schools which exist within that polity ($r = 0.57$). It is considerably less covariant, in the smaller sample for which data are available, with the percentage of the governmental budget devoted to education (0.25). There are several discrepancies, other than those noted above, which may serve to contaminate this latter correlation. First and foremost among them is the fact that this correlation is based upon a sample of sixty-four polities which largely excludes non-market economies and underdeveloped nations. Furthermore, the adopted measure is not unrelated to the mass education programs in general, since widespread education is prerequisite for the existence of a large number of universities, although it is quite possible for a small number of universities to be fuelled by elitist educational systems which do not extend education to the masses. The contrary is exceedingly unlikely. Such an operational indicator does not allow the assessment of educational equality, however. In spite of its shortcomings, the number of universities seems like a reasonable, if imperfect, indicator.

While the number of possible policy efforts which might profitably be investigated here is large, these two will suffice for the examination to follow. Thus, general social welfare policy and educational policy will serve as the primary indicators of policy efforts at redistribution.

4.4 POLITICAL MOBILIZATION AND POLICY DEMAND

Many arguments about the plight of inequality in the historical evolution of a polity are greatly attuned to the degree of awareness, participation, and organization of the "masses." The many strains of this argument go something like this: as a political structure begins to become more economically developed, there is a basic change in the structure of the population not only in terms of its geographic location (i.e., urban rather than rural) and mode of economic production (i.e., industrial rather than agricultural), but also in general outlook—in terms of self and others. Lerner's early work (1958) framed this change in a world view which associated changes in the communication patterns of individual and group members of the "modernizing" society, but others have carried forth this theoretical argument in much more recent research. This tradition is also closely related to Karl W. Deutsch's contribution to the whole of social science on the relation of cybernetic theory to social organization (1961, 1966a, and 1966b). Furthermore, the argument goes, this change in world view is accompanied, and indeed partially caused, by an increased volume of such information available in more "modernized" societies. The basic tenets of this argument have been widely adopted by social scientists who have focused their attention on the process and consequences of modernization in developing nations (*a la* Lerner) as well as developing cities.

The implication of such an argument for the present study is twofold. First, it brings into greater focus the political and social factors which scholars like Kuznets, among others, have alluded to as the reason for a leveling off of the impact of economic development on equality. Specifically, the argument implies that as more people become aware and involved in the political process they will make increased demands upon the distributive mechanisms of that structure. These demands may lead to increased satisfaction or to increased dissatisfaction, depending upon whether or not they are met. This leads to the second implication, which suggests the types of mechanisms that themselves lead to the origination of policy effort in the area of distributional planning. Thus, it focuses attention on the question of why redistributive policies are attempted and what forces may account for their origin.

Most of the empirical work in this area has been done from the framework of pluralist democratic structures and competitive political processes. Specifically, the notion has been that increased awareness, itself primarily caused by increased social communication and mobilization which is concomitant with economic development, leads to increased participation in the decision-making process through competitive forces such as interest groups, labor unions, and political parties. This increased participation is channeled through these organizations in such a manner as to translate the predispositions of the mass to the decision-making elite—which itself is often isomorphic with the elite of the mass organizations (Michels, 1915). Thus, it is often argued, increased mobilization leads to increased participation, which in turn leads to increased demands upon the decision-making structure.

A second source of policy effort has its etiology not in the mass political movements which arise in the development process, but rather in the origin of ideological movements which have aimed at translating the redistributive ideas of Marx and Lenin (among others) into social policy with or without the stimulus of mass participation in competitive political processes. Thumbnail sketches of these two large and complex political orientations cannot do justice to either. However, the present purpose is not to explore the larger differences between democratic and nondemocratic political structures and processes. Instead, these two political styles are explored for the ways in which each may lead to policy effort directed at the (re)distribution of social welfare. Such sketches do provide the necessary context for explorations of this sort. The basic argument posed here is that policy effort arises out of the awareness of the policy making elite; this awareness presumably can be stimulated by several factors, including mass participation in the political process at the level of initiating demands as well as a more ideological commitment toward policy effort in certain areas, such as the redistribution of social product. The level of such stimulation defines, for present purposes, the level of political mobilization.

From the pluralist perspective, several different aspects of political mobilization and participation are important to the overall argument. Two of the most prominent of these have been drawn from social communication theories of political mobilization: participation and openness. The overriding conceptual picture is that not only should there be opportunities for participation (channels in the language of Weiner [1948] and more recently Gurr [1974]), but these channels should be used frequently. Gurr's work in erecting typologies of the authority characteristics of polities is useful in the present effort not only for the conceptual picture it paints of the structure of openness in a polity's channels and the behavioral use of such structures, but also because it provides operational indicators for each of these two concepts. These two indices as well as an aggregate index of the extent of democracy (DEMOC) which a polity exhibits are defined in Table 4.3. The democracy index combines several of the salient authority characteristics of a polity into one score. Among these characteristics, deemed important in democratic political structures, are the openness and participation as well as the centralization of power, constraints placed upon the top decision makers by other elected bodies, and the extent to which elite recruitment is elective. As defined and operationalized, such an index (DEMOC) gauges not only the extent or channels of competition and openness which are structured in political systems, but also the amount of participation which exists within them. For pluralist-competitive systems this index should serve as an appropriate indicator of the political mobilization. The actual codings for the polities in the present study were taken from the original study done by Gurr of over four-hundred historical and contemporary polities.

TABLE 4.3. *Operational Definitions of the Openness of Elite Recruitment, Extent of Political Competition and Opposition, and Democracy**

Recruitment: Openness of Executive Selection

TYPE OF SELECTION	OPENNESS SCORE
Competitive	5
Caesaristic	4
Dual executive	3
Designation	2
Ascription	1

Participation: Extent of Political Competition and Opposition

PATTERN OF COMPETITION	PARTICIPATION SCORE
Institutionalized	5
Factional/restricted	4
Uninstitutionalized	3
Restricted	2
Suppressed or nonexistent	1

Democracy Components: Score

Competitive elections	2
Institutionalized competition	2
Executive independence	
Legislative parity	2
Substantial limits	1
Decentralized power	1

Democracy score = Sum of democracy components scores

* Tables 1 (p. 1485) and 2 (p. 1487) in T. R. Gurr (1974), "Persistence and Change in Political Systems, 1800–1971," *American Political Science Review,* 68, No. 4, 1482–1505, provided the basis for the above table. A more extensive discussion of the coding of the variables is contained therein. The actual scores used in this study were also taken from Gurr's study.

The possible indicators of ideological commitment to welfare policy which is conducted irrespective of participation in open, competitive political processes are similarly difficult to measure. A list of potential, and vastly imperfect, indicators includes the strength of the communist party, the degree of nonmarket organization of the economy, the degree of autocracy, and the legal status of the communist party. Arbitrarily, the strength of the communist party in terms of the percentage of the population was chosen as the operational indicator. This choice was predicated on the fact that while some noncommunist polities have sizable communist parties, the size of the communist party does tend to set apart the communist bloc from socialist polities. For example, the size of the communist party ranges roughly from about four or five percent in the Soviet Union to about thirteen percent in North Korea which is conventionally regarded as having the most extensive communist party organization relative to its size. The separation of communist from socialist polities—and recognizably these distinctions are controversial—was made with the notion that socialist polities are still much more characterized by competitive processes. Thus, while there is strong ideological commitment to social ideals, as also may exist in democratic polities, similar in kind to that in communist societies, the similarities to democratic processes were much greater than to the more totalitarian ones. The size of the communist party in nonpluralist polities tends to reflect the organizational strength of the elite decision making body. As such it should, if arguments posed here are relatively valid, also indicate the extent of political mobilization in the sense that larger parties tend to indicate a larger and more complicated elite structure. Since this elite structure is viewed as initiating most if not all of the explicit demands in noncompetitive polities, the relative size of the communist party was chosen as the operational indicator of political mobilization in noncompetitive polities.

The two indices outlined above, the democracy score and the size of the communist party, tend to be unrelated to one another, except that polities with a high score in one index usually have a negligible score in the other. In that sense these two operate much like dummy variables. They were Z-scored, and additively combined to create the operational indicator of political mobilization in all polities (POLMOB). Thus, this transformation was chosen so that a polity with a high score on either index would receive a high mobilization score, while a polity with a low score on both would receive a low mobilization score.

Having laid the theoretical groundwork of the model to be examined in this chapter, as well as having chosen empirical indicators which operationalize the relevant concepts used, the next step is to formalize the model in logical and mathematical terms, and to evaluate its empirical validity. This will be accomplished in section 4.5.

4.5 FORMALIZATION AND EVALUATION OF THE MODEL

On the basis of the economic arguments in the previous chapter as well as the more political arguments presented in the present chapter, it is relatively straightforward to formalize the model of the internal determinants of inequality. This formalization may proceed along lines which are purely logical, mathematical, or both. In axiomatic terms, the model has three basic components or axioms. These postulates are interrelated in the form of a logical structure, i.e., syllogism or theory, which states that the level of inequality within a contemporary polity is a direct function of the resources available to that polity, the degree of effort which is undertaken to retard inequality, and the level of political awareness and mobilization which is directed toward such goals. The following logical structure is posited:

A1. Equality requires moderate wealth.
   $E \rightarrow W$. (Should be read "if E, then W").

A2. Without policy effort, moderate wealth is unlikely to bring about equality. Thus, equality will not occur without policy effort.
   $-P \rightarrow -E$. ("if not P, then not E")

A3. Policy effort is unlikely to occur without political mobilization.
   $-M \rightarrow -P$.

Utilizing the laws of logic, it is relatively simple to derive from these three axioms the general and abstract conclusion that represents the thrust of the theory presented here: namely, that equality is a function of wealth, policy effort, and political mobilization.

Specifically, by the contraposition of A2 and A3, it follows that:

Theorem 1. $\therefore E \rightarrow P$, and
Theorem 2. $\therefore P \rightarrow M$.

By the rule of hypothetical syllogism (H.S.), it also follows that:

Theorem 3 $\therefore E \rightarrow M$.
   (H.S. on TH1 and TH2)

Further, by material implication (Impl.) on A1, Th1, and Th3, it is seen that:

Theorem 4. $\therefore$ -E v M. (Impl.)
                (read "not E or M")
Theorem 5. $\therefore$ -E v P, (Impl.)
Theorem 6. $\therefore$ -E v W (Impl.)

By the rule of distribution (D), Theorem 7 may be stated as follows:

Theorem 7. $\therefore$ -E v (M$\cdot$P$\cdot$W) (D.)
                (read "not E or M and P and W")

Finally, by material implication and double negation (D.N.), it is proved that:

Theorem 8. $\therefore$ E $\rightarrow$ (M$\cdot$P$\cdot$W)
                (Impl.) and (D.N.)

Verbally this theorem, which is proved in symbolic form above, states that if the axioms are true, then political mobilization, social welfare policy efforts, and wealth are necessary for the possession and maintenance of equality as defined herein. The obvious corollary is that without each of these elements, society is unlikely to (re)distribute social product in an egalitarian fashion. Note that this theory does not explicitly concern itself with the *generation* of inequality or equality; rather, it is a theory about the level of inequality that is likely to be exhibited by polities which have varying degrees of wealth, policy effort, and political mobilization.

This general model can be further recast in light of the conceptual variables and their operationalizations developed above. Such effort necessarily builds upon the results of the previous chapters; accordingly, the same symbolism is adopted. Mathematically, this operationalized model can be represented by three equations which are themselves interrelated. These are presented in equations (4.2) through (4.4):

(4.2) $X4 = \alpha + \beta_1 X1 + \beta_2 X6$

(4.3) $X5 = \alpha + \beta_1 X1 + \beta_2 X6$

(4.4) $Y = \alpha + \beta_1 X2 + \beta_2 X2 \cdot X3 + \beta_3 X4 + \beta_4 X5$

Where: Y = Inequality index
           X1 = Energy consumption *per capita*
           X2 = Index of construction activity
           X3 = Index of economic diversity
           X4 = Index of educational policy effort
           X5 = Index of general welfare policy effort
           X6 = Index of political mobilization

These equations may now be used to construct an evaluation of the model via regression analysis. In this particular case, since no feedback is postulated, ordinary least squares (OLS) is appropriate.

As discussed before, the specification of the form of the relationship between economic development and inequality was posited to be curvilinear. Furthermore, it is suggested on theoretical and empirical grounds that a logarithmic specification of that relationship was most appropriate. What has been highlighted here is that the bulk of the argument for such a curvilinear relationship in the first place was based upon the fact that explicitly political factors were omitted from the model. The curvilinearity was posited to replace the impact of these factors—or at least to replace their conglomerate effect. Both a linear and curvilinear specification is tested upon the model as presented in equations (4.2) through (4.4).

The OLS results for this model which is represented by the above equations, (4.2) through (4.4), are given in Table 4.4.

With respect to the comparison of the relative appropriateness of curvilinear *versus* linear specifications of the link between economic development and inequality, and in light of the inclusion of political factors, it may be observed that the linear form provides a much better empirical and theoretical fit. The increase in $\overline{R2}$ and path coefficients is substantial and significant in both equations (4.2) and (4.3). Respectively, $\overline{R2}$ increases from 0.16 to 0.45 and from 0.18 to 0.23 in these equations. The path coefficients for the linear model are much stronger than the curvilinear model. Specifically, in the case of educational policy, the coefficient is more than doubled in the linear as opposed to curvilinear specification (0.76 *versus* 0.26); the increase in the path coefficient of the impact of economic development on unemployment policy is less dramatic, although the increase is substantial (0.47 from 0.33). Thus, now that no overriding theoretical reasons exist for retaining a surrogate curvilinear relationship between economic development and inequality, and since some of the important political elements

TABLE 4.4. *Estimation of Model Hypothesizing Subnational Determinants of Inequality Using Linear and Curvilinear Specifications of the Relationship Between Economic Development and Inequality*[a]

INDEPENDENT VARIABLE	REGRESSION COEFFICIENT		STANDARD ERROR		STANDARDIZED COEFFICIENT	
	Linear	Curvi-linear	Linear	Curvi-linear	Linear	Curvi-linear
Equation (4.2)	Dependent Variable : UNEMFAC					
ENGCON	33.10*	(.25*)	8.3	(.08)	.47	(.33)
POLMOB	.02	(.16)	.13	(.13)	.02	(.14)
Equation (4.3)	Dependent Variable : UNVRSTY					
ENGCON	385.57*	(1.38*)	50.5	(.60)	.76	(.26)
POLMOB	−1.32	(1.68)	.81	(.90)	−.16	(.20)
Equation (4.4)	Dependent Variable : INEQUAL					
INTERACT	−2.82*		.73		−.70	
UNVRSTY	−.02*		.01		−.33	
UNEMFAC	−.12*		.05		−.27	
IXCONS	.01*		.001		.59	

Equation	R2		$\overline{R2}$		F		p=		DF[b]
(4.2)	.23	(.18)	.21	(.17)	14.7	(10.9)	.000	(.000)	98 (98)
(4.3)	.45	(.16)	.44	(.15)	36.9	(9.6)	.000	(.000)	98 (98)
(4.4)	.50		.46		13.4		.000		56

* Statistically significant at the 0.05 level or better.

a. Where:
  INEQUAL = Inequality index (Y)
  ENGCON = Energy consumption per capita (X1)
  POLMOB = Political mobilization score (X6)
  INTERACT = Interaction of IXCONS (X2) and the diversity of the economic structure (X3)
  UNVRSTY = Index of educational policy (X4)
  UNEMFAC = Index of welfare policy (X5)
  IXCONS = Index of short-term economic growth (X2)

For extensive defiitions, see Appendix B.

b. Significance is based upon the smallest N from the individual correlations. Most coefficients are based on over 100 cases.

have been included, the linear relationship gives a much improved empirical and theoretical fit over the previous curvilinear form.

In terms of the overall fit of the estimated model to the theory, it appears that two of the three postulated links have been upheld (or may not be rejected). The link between resources (X1) and policy variables (X4 and X5) is strong and stable. The second major link, between policy variables coupled with the economic structure identified earlier (X2 and X2·X3) and inequality (Y), is also strong, significant, and in the predicted direction in each instance. The second link, seen in equation (4.4), is strongly represented by the OLS estimates and explains almost half of the total variation in inequality ($\overline{R2}$ = 0.46).The third one, however produces more "problematic" results. This link illustrates the relationship between political mobilization, X6, and the two policy variables, X4 and X5. None of these coefficients is significant; in the linear specification the path coefficients are in the opposite sign than the one predicted. Leaving behind the curvilinear specification, the results of the OLS estimation of the model are investigated.

In general, the model and the data show remarkable correspondence. The link between economic development and inequality which was established previously is seen to be stable in light of the introduction of other influences, which are primarily political, into the equation set. The linkages between these economic variables and inequality are, however, basically unchanged by this more complete specification. This may be taken as an indication that the residual variance is partially explained by the political variables. In fact, the two policy indicators, educational policy (X4) and social welfare policy (X5), are themselves strongly related to inequality in the predicted direction. Considering these two links alone, then, the picture suggested by the theoretical model and the data are relatively isomorphic. Stated simply, policy variables represent an important set of intervening variables which mediate the relationship between economic development and the level of inequality within contemporary polities.

While the overall fit between the model and the data is strong, in that the OLS results increase the plausibility of two of the basic links suggested, the lack of complete correspondence with respect to the stimulus of policy effort is itself worthy of comment. One interpretation, the most evident, is that political mobilization has no positive impact on the generation of policy effort in the area of distributional planning which is independent of the impact of the level of economic development. In fact, based upon the data analysis, it appears that the

[109]

level of political mobilization tends to exhibit a dampening effect on educational policy. While these interpretations may seem counterintuitive, that alone is grossly insufficient for their rejection. On the other hand, their acceptance brings into question the overall theory proposed above, entailing as it does a modification if not a rejection of one of the axioms. However, it must be emphasized that the axiom involved is not an ultimately crucial one in the sense that without it the entire theory would collaspe. That is not the case, for without the assumption about the genesis of policy effort, the theory becomes less extensive, but the basic conclusion would remain relatively unchanged. It would simply imply that the level of inequality is a function of resources and policy effort alone. Before accepting this diminution of the scope of the theory, it is important to scrutinize more carefully the findings presented in Table 4.5 for possible rival explanations which might account for the results.

There are several plausible explanations for the lack of empirical accord between the data and the model in regard to the political mobilization variables. The indicators which are imperfect at best may possibly be biased in such a fashion as to obscure the "real" underlying relationships. For example, the chosen indicator of political mobilization in communist nations (the percentage of the population belonging to an organized communist party) holds several recognized pitfalls, notably the fact that size, organizational skill, and ideological commitment are not isomorphic. Several other indicators including the strength of the communist party as estimated by the U. S. State Department (1975) [2 = communist party is legal and in power. 1 = communist party is legal but not in power, and 0 = communist party is illegal], a dummy variable for the extent of nonmarket organization of the economy, the raw size of the communist party, and several other operationalizations of this variable were substituted for the one chosen above. In every case, the results were roughly isomorphic to those presented above: there was no significant positive relationship between political mobilization as measured in noncompetitive polities and policy effort.

Another rival explanation deals not with the mobilization indices themselves, but with the policy indicators. One particular source of trouble in these operationalizations is the extent to which the unemployment index is an appropriate indicator for polities with nonmarket organization of their economic systems. Communist countries

TABLE 4.5. *Estimation of the Revised Model of the Internal Determinants of Inequality in the Contemporary Polity*[a]

INDEPENDENT VARIABLE	REGRESSION COEFFICIENT	STANDARD ERROR	STANDARDIZED COEFFICIENT
Equation (4.2)	Dependent Variable : UNEMFAC		
ENGCON	33.86*	5.8	.48
Equation (4.3)	Dependent Variable : UNVRSTY		
ENGCON	331.23*	35.28	.66
Equation (4.4)	Dependent Variable : INEQUAL		
INTERACT	−2.82*	.73	−.70
UNVRSTY	−.02*	.01	−.33
UNEMFAC	−.12*	.05	−.27
IXCONS	.01*	.001	.59

Equation	R2	$\overline{R2}$	F	p=	DF[b]
(4.2)	.23	.22	33.8	.000	113
(4.3)	.43	.43	88.2	.000	116
(4.4)	.50	.46	13.4	.000	56

* Statistically significant at the 0.05 level or better.

a. Where:
    INEQUAL = Inequality index (Y)
    ENGCON = Energy consumption per capita (X1)
    INTERACT = Interaction of IXCONS (X2), and the diversity of the economic structure (X3)
    UNVRSTY = Index of educational policy (X4)
    UNEMFAC = Index of welfare policy (X5)
    IXCONS = Index of short-term economic growth (X2)
For extensive definitions, see Appendix B.

b. Significance is based upon the smallest N from the individual correlations. Most coefficients are based on over 100 cases.

in particular often tend to handle "unemployment" in an altogether different way than socialist or capitalist countries. Thus, the lack of a social security program for unemployment might not indicate the absence of a high level of governmental policy aimed at full employment. However, it is not impossible for communist countries to have unemployment programs; East Germany and Poland, for example, as well as others, have relatively strong unemployment programs. A large number of the communist countries do not have any program that is currently recognized by the U.S. Social Security Administration. This potentially biases the results; however, it should be kept in mind that the unemployment program index was chosen because it was the most difficult, in a scaling sense, to achieve. On the whole, the lack of unemployment programs may be indicative of either a shortcoming in the index construction or of a lower level of policy intervention in communist as opposed to socialist and capitalist polities.

Two further interpretations will be explored. Simply, one is that economic development is more important than political style in eliciting policy effort. From a statistical standpoint this could be attributed to multicollinearity between economic development and political mobilization, but then can be cautiously rejected, since the Pearson correlation is only 0.3. Substantively, it could be that these mobilization forces are relatively unimportant. The other interpretation is that some combination of the potential contaminating forces explored above is responsible for the results which are catalogued in Table 4.4. Since alternative indices were introduced above and proved to be substantially equivalent to those initially chosen, it seems impossible to resolve this difficulty here.

On the basis of evidence presented here, however, it appears that policy effort is not greatly effected by political mobilization. Accordingly, the model was reestimated, deleting the link between political mobilization and policy effort. The results of this estimation are presented in Table 4.5 and Figure 4.1.

The interpretation of the results produced in Table 4.5 is rather straightforward. Each of the postulated links are seen to bear substantial support in the data analyzed. It must not be forgotten, however, that the link between political mobilization and policy efforts has been left out because of a lack of fit. The deletion of this link produces results which are not dissimilar from those produced earlier in Table 4.4, thus vindicating the deletion on empirical, though not theoretical grounds. The parsed model presents a robust representation of the empirical relationships extant in the data analyzed: inequality tends to be increased by short-term economic growth and decreased by policy efforts in education and unemployment; policy efforts themselves tend to be associated with high levels of economic growth, thus suggesting an indirect link between the level of economic development and the level of inequality.

The estimation of all components of the model met with relative

FIGURE 4.1. Schematic Representation of the Linkages Among the
Development Process, Policy Effort, and Inequality[a]

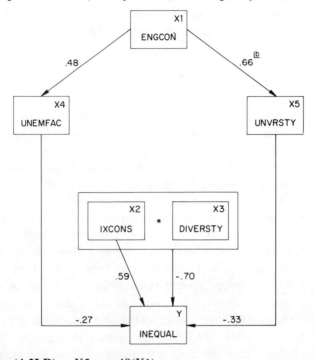

Equation (4.2LR)   X5 = .48(X1)

$\overline{R2}^c$ = .22   F = 33.8   p ≤ .000

Equation (4.3LR)   X4 = .66(X1)

$\overline{R2}$ = .43   F = 88.2   p ≤ .000

Equation (4.4LR)   Y = .59(X2) − .70(X2·X3) − .33(X4) − .27(X5)

$\overline{R2}$ = .50   F = 13.4   p ≤ .000

---

a. Where: INEQUAL   (Y) = Composite inequality index
              ENGCON   (X1) = Energy consumption per capita
              IXCONS   (X2) = Index of construction activity
             DIVERSTY (X3) = Index of the diversity of the economic infrastructure
             UNVRSTY   (X4) = Index of educational policy effort
             UNEMFAC   (X5) = Index of unemployment policy effort
    These variables and their components are explained in greater detail in Appendix B, wherein reference is
    made to their introduction into the text.
b. Standardized regression coefficients are reported. For more complete information on estimation, see
    Table 4.6. All estimates are statistically significant at the 0.05 level or better.
c. Corrected coefficient of determination is equivalent to the percent of variance in the dependent variable
    which is explained by the independent variables.
*   This symbol represents multiplicative interaction.

success, and while the prediction of values for the main dependent variable, inequality, was fairly accurate (roughly half of the total variance was explained), it is equally important to examine in detail the discrepancies between the predicted and the actual values in such estimations. Table 4.6 presents the values of the inequality index, the estimated values based upon equation (4.4), and the residuals for each of the 120 polities in the sample. Note that missing data were estimated (based upon the weighted mean of the individual distributions) whenever 75 per cent of the data were available on any individual case. This means that estimates were generated only in cases where there was data on three of the four independent variables in this equation. Such a conservative procedure for estimation of missing data has the payoff of generating values for each of the 120 cases.

Neither statistical nor visual analysis of the residuals revealed any glaring irregularities. Less than eight per cent of cases had residuals that were two standard deviations away from the estimated line. Of those extreme outliers, four were cases in which the equation "underestimated" the inequality. Three of these four cases, Upper Volta, Liberia, and Afghanistan, have extremely high values for the index of inequality. Five cases were estimated to have less inequality than would be predicted by their values on the four independent variables. Each of these five cases are European polities, Austria, Switzerland, Bulgaria, Poland, and Romania, and three of these are communist nations. Furthermore, it should be pointed out that the richer countries tend to have less observed inequality than would be predicted by the model, while in poorer countries there is more inequality than predicted. Thus, several areas for additional analysis are suggested. The most striking of these is the still wide gap between rich and poor nations. Another potentially fruitful area is that of the impact of socialist revolutions, inasmuch as communist nations all tend to have moderately large negative residual scores, indicating the inadequacy of the model for these polities.

4.6 SUMMARY

 . Theoretically and empirically, this chapter has shown that a major part of any explanation of the inequality within contemporary polities must include the resources available to the polity, as well as the extent

TABLE 4.6. *Predicted (Ŷ) and Residual (e) Inequality Scores from Estimation of Equation (4.4), Arranged by Level of Gross National Product Per Capita**

Greater than $1200

NATION	Ŷ	e
USA	-181	43
SWE	-12	-57
CAN	-85	-97
ICE	-41	35
SWI	-33	-132
LUX	-41	-65
FRN	-80	-15
DEN	-22	-63
NOR	-33	-29
GMW	-81	73
AUL	-62	-31
IRE	-45	52
BEL	-19	-89
NET	0	-92
UNK	-70	-27
CZE	-33	-85
USR	-41	-61
FIN	-50	-37
GME	-68	-33
PUE	18	-46
ISR	-46	-42
NEW	-48	-33
AUS	0	-109
JAP	-133	83
ITA	-53	-69
HUN	-0	-94
POL	0	-100

Between $1200 and $300

NATION	Ŷ	e	NATION	Ŷ	e
ROM	29	-117	HOK	-0	29
VEN	0	17	ALB	53	-41
BUL	11	-105	JOR	0	32
GRC	-0	-84	PAR	42	-10
SPA	0	-36	TUR	57	-89
SAF	0	17	HON	59	45
LEB	35	-16	GUA	45	24
CHI	-19	24	BHO	19	27
URU	-0	-39	MLY	13	16
ANG	-0	-83	PER	17	32
CUB	17	-28	BRA	-20	42
MEX	33	30	CHT	14	-29
COS	28	-25	IRQ	33	29
SAU	-16	10	IRN	29	42
YUG	31	-56	COL	22	13
PAN	31	91	ELS	44	24
POR	0	-40	SEN	18	37
JAM	28	11	GUI	33	90
NIC	37	49			

Less than $300

NATION	Ŷ	e	NATION	Ŷ	e
IVO	31	94	ETH	-0	39
DOM	71	-22	NIG	32	-44
ZAM	10	34	IND	36	74
GHA	21	34	NGA	67	-19
KON	28	76	TAN	105	-48
KOS	74	-66	BUR	37	11
ALG	72	29	BOT	222	-73
PHI	-17	57	VOL	18	101
TUN	25	65	SIN	20	-21
BOL	111	-94	ZAI	15	80
MRC	43	15	MLW	20	33
ZIM	17	31	BRD	31	-41
EGY	-0	31	CAR	26	39
CAO	41	33	CEY	57	-33
TAI	36	-49	CHA	17	26
VTS	18	58	CON	34	81
SYR	41	-59	CYP	-0	59
ECU	17	81	DAH	23	17
CAM	22	41	GAB	15	47
MGY	32	19	GAM	22	28
SUD	19	44	LAO	22	25
AFG	0	112	LES	28	-36
PAK	48	-42	LIB	20	102
CHN	54	-26	SIE	20	35
LBY	-71	107	SOM	20	68
UGA	0	27	YES	28	61
YEN	28	65			
VTN	25	35			
KEN	47	10			
INS	20	73			

* Scores have been multiplied by 100 to remove the decimal.

and success of its policy efforts aimed at effecting redistribution. The level of political awareness and mobilization which was argued to stimulate that policy effort was found to be unrelated to such effort in the group of nations analyzed herein. Polities which exhibit a low level of any of these two variables tend to have more inequality than those that have higher levels of resources and policy effort. In terms of the causal hierarchy among these components of the explanatory framework, the role of the economic structure and the role of the policy efforts are apparently more important than the level of political mobilization alone. It is hard to accept these negative results, inasmuch as it seems so plausible that the existence of policy effort itself is sufficient demonstration of political awareness and mobilization toward collective goals.

One major area of internal politics which, lamentably, has been excluded from the present analysis deals not with the causes of inequality, but rather with the effects of varying levels of inequality upon other social processes within the polity. It is a question of overwhelming importance: What are the consequences of high levels of inequality? Many have argued that high inequality leads almost directly to a heightened propensity for mass violence, while others have argued that inequalities are evaluated in relative terms. Furthermore, even if the direct consequences of inequality are minimal, these consequences themselves may have feedback or secondary effects with great impact on the stability of the system in economic as well as political realms. For example, large scale mass political violence is very likely to prove disruptive for the economic structure. This in turn may effect the level of inequality within a polity. Unfortunately, such interesting questions must be set aside for the time being.

If the arguments presented here are correct, the search for the determinants of inequality is incomplete with a consideration of the international phenomena which impinges upon the internal behavior of political systems. The present investigation now proceeds toward this endeavor.

R E F E R E N C E S

Adelman, I. and C. Morris (1973). Economic Growth and Social Equity in Developing Countries. Stanford: Stanford University Press.
Boudon, R. (1974). Education Opportunities, and Social Inequality: Changing Pros-

[116]

pects in Western Society, a translation of *L'inegalite des Chances,* by the author. New York: John Wiley.

Buchanan, J. (1968). The Demand and Supply of Public Goods. Chicago, Illinois: Rand-McNally.

Chenery, H., S. Ahluwalia, C. L. G. Bell, J. H. Duloy, and R. Jolly (1974). Redistribution with Growth. New York: Oxford University Press.

Chenery, H., M. Syrquin, with H. Elkington (1975). Patterns of Development, 1950-1970. New York: Oxford University Press.

Chiswick, B. R. (1974). Income Inequality: Regional Analysis within a Human Capital Framework. NBER, New York: Columbia University Press.

Cutright, P. (1965). "Political Structure, Economic Development, and National Social Security Programs." American Journal of Sociology, Vol. 70, pp 537-550.

Cutright, P. (1967). "Inequality: A Cross-National Analysis." American Sociological Review, Vol. 32, pp 562-578.

Deutsch, K. W. (1961). "Social Mobilization and Political Development." The American Political Science Review, Vol. 55, No. 3, pp 493-514.

Deutsch, K. W. (1966a). The Nerves of Government, 2nd edition. New York: Free Press.

Deutsch, K. W. (1966b). Nationalism and Social Communication, revised edition. Cambridge, Mass.: MIT Press.

Echols, J. (1975). "Politics, Budgets, and Regional Equality in Communist and Capitalist Systems." Comparative Political Studies, Vol. 8, No. 3, pp 259-292.

Gurr, T. R. (1974). "Persistence and Change in Political Systems, 1860-1971." American Political Science Review, Vol. 68, No. 4, pp 1482-1505.

Jackman, R. W. (1975). Politics and Social Equality. New York: John Wiley.

Jencks, C., et al. (1972). Inequality: A Reassessment of the Effect of Family and Schooling in America. New York: Basic Books.

Kuznets, S. (1955). "Economic Growth and Income Inequality." American Economic Review, Vol. 45, pp 1-28.

Kuznets, S. (1963). "Quantitative Aspects of the Economic Growth of Nations, VIII: The Distribution of Income by Size." Economic Development and Cultural Change, Vol. 11, part 2 (entire).

Lerner, D. (1956). The Passing of Traditional Society. New York: Free Press.

Michels, R. (1915). Political Parties: A Sociological Study of the Oligarchical Tendencies of Modern Democracy. New York: Dover Publications, 1959.

Marshall, A. (1920). Industry and Trade. London: The Macmillan Company.

Marshall, A. (1952). Principles of Economics, 8th edition. London: The Macmillan Company.

Olson, M. (1965). The Logic of Collective Action. Cambridge, Mass.: Harvard University Press.

Social Security Programs Throughout the World, 1973 (1973). Research Report No. 44. The Social Security Administration, Washington, D.C.

Weiner, N. (1948). Cybernetics. New York: John Wiley.

Wilensky, H. (1975). The Welfare State and Equality: Structural and Ideological Roots of Public Expenditures. Berkeley, California: The University of California Press.

Yotopolous, P. and J. Nugent (1976). Economics of Development: Empirical Investigations. New York: Harper and Row.

[117]

International Determinants of Inequality: A Structural Approach

5

5.1 INTRODUCTION

Given the picture presented in the previous chapters on the relation between economic structure and economic progress and the level of inequality in the distribution of material goods in contemporary polities, the prognosis for increased levels of development and consequently, in the long run, reduced levels of inequality should be encouraging for those who value greater levels of material well-being for more of the world's inhabitants. To a greater or lesser extent, societies with high levels of inequality can bring about lower levels of inequality for the most part by increasing productivity and formulating policies aimed at redistribution. High levels of development are viewed as indicative if not provocative of higher levels of equality and lower levels of unequal distributions of material goods. If such a picture is promising or encouraging in the mid-1970s, it certainly must have led to much of the unchecked optimism of the early 1950s. However, the success of the Third World countries in developing has justifiably tended to erode faith in the unseen hand of economic development. Moreover, to the extent that development has been achieved, historical experience has shown that the translation of newly cultivated levels of productivity into more equality has not been uniform in either extent or direction.

There are, of course, several important successes which have fueled the confidence many hold in development. Taiwan, South Korea, and

Sri Lanka, among others, have been offered as prime recent examples of how development can raise productivity and, when coupled with policy efforts, thereby effect significant redistributions of economic product within an increasingly developed economic and political structure. On the other hand, there are at least as many overwhelming failures; nations which have undertaken the same *genre* of policies and which have neither achieved a significantly higher level of development nor an increase in the level of equality present within those polities. Even more confounding is the argument posed by many scholars that the pursuit of the "neoclassical" development strategy has itself tended to aggravate not only the underdevelopment, but also the inequality of the Third World polities. At the very least, these factors suggest that the theoretical perspective is incomplete inasmuch as there are a large number of cases that cannot be explained by reference to such ideas as those posed in the neoclassical model. More critically, it is certainly plausible that the entire perspective needs a serious revamping, if not dismissal.

International factors have consciously been omitted from the foregoing analyses, and since it has become increasingly apparent that from a multitude of perspectives the "underdeveloped" polity cannot easily solve economic problems within a purely national framework, the viability of the domestic perspective on development and equality cannot stand much scrutiny without inclusion of the international (external) factors which also impinge upon the characteristics, strategies, and policies of both developing and industrialized polities. This chapter adopts as its rationale the development of a theory which incorporates such international factors into the model developed in the previous chapters. The concepts of hierarchical position and interaction and system monitoring will be utilized as the primary international factors in affecting differential patterns of inequality within contemporary polities.

5.2 HIERARCHY: POSITION, INTERACTION, AND MONITORING

International relations, with many other disciplines across the gamut of social sciences, has turned much of its recent attention to the study of what have come to be known as structural questions. This is true with respect to epistemology, i.e., structuralism as a paradigm, of many scholars as well as the empirical focus of many others, i.e., structuralism as a dependent and/or independent "variable." The myriad works of Piaget (1970) have stimulated much of this multidisciplinary interest, and the early works of Marx and Lenin provide a powerful touchstone for comprehending the works of more modern "Marxist-Leninist" political economists. Latin American "dependency" theorists such as Furtado, Dos Santos, and Sunkel, among others, surely have provided the most recent powerful impetus stimulating the attention international relations have begun to show in structural questions.

The intellectual roots of this newborn attention could profitably be traced, but most properly the movement began with the attempts of Latin American economists to understand rather concrete policy questions. Specifically, at issue was the status of the development of several Latin American economies. The United Nations self-proclaimed decade(s) of development eventuated without much impact. During the early 1950s, studies were undertaken at the UN which were to presage this development. A group of economists, which later came to be known as the Prebisch school, began to devote attention to the path of Latin American economic development. Succinctly, they uncovered considerable evidence which brought into question the long-standing economic principles of exchange theory and comparative advantage. Based upon these researches, there developed a flurry of ideological and theoretical activity. This has been named "dependency theory" by some. While this theory is very diverse and multifaceted, as well as self-contradictory, it provides a touchstone for understanding the work of many modern international relations scholars working in the *milieu* of structuralism. Virtually all studies make reference to the seminal works of Latin American scholars such as Sunkel (1969), Furtado (1970), and Dos Santos (1970). Similarly, most of the recent empirical and theoretical activity implicitly uses various concepts and propositions drawn from the "*dependencia*" literature. At least one recent study argues that the bulk of dependency literature may be viewed as representing enough consistency and focus to be considered as a theory of imperialism that is subject to empirical examination (Duvall and Russett, 1976).

Western attention from scholarly and policy perspectives has also been stimulated by the contemporary "energy crisis" and the ascendency of several previously "dependent" polities. The question has largely been defined in terms of what is the "structure" of relationships among units in the international systems such that some polities are persistently "on top" and others are persistently "on bottom"? (Galtung, 1971). With the ascendency of several OPEC countries, this question has been reformulated into more specific queries: (1) will those previously dominant become dominated in the near future, i.e., dependent, and (2) what is the process whereby dependency can be either eliminated or reversed? Most stimulating theoretical work on these questions has come from the pens of Walter Buckley, Tom Baumgartner, and Tom Burns (1975a, 1975b, 1976). These works build upon the system theoretic work of Walter Buckley (1967), and additionally incorporate several structural arguments which have been developed to interface economic and political decision-making. Much of what follows owes a great intellectual debt to the works of Buckley and his associates. The overriding framework is, however, based upon the question of how goods such as power, position, and interaction are distributed in the international system, and how that distribution is related to the internal distribution of goods within the individual polities which comprise part of that international system.

Early attempts to understand the structure of the international system have used the notion of hierarchy in ways which were often more implicit (e.g., Kaplan, 1957) than explicit (e.g., Brams, 1966). In asserting that politics should be equated with authority relations, Eckstein and Gurr (1975) have definitionally incorporated the notion of hierarchy into the concept of authority relations (and presumably, politics):

> An authority pattern is a set of asymmetric relations among hierarchically ordered members of a social unit that involves the direction of the unit. . . . Hierarchic order exists where members of a unit are perceived as ranked in levels of superiority and inferiority [1975:22].

In general, the definition of hierarchy incorporates the notion of authority. Within this more conventional framework, there are at least two rather divergent interpretations of what is meant by the term "hierarchy." One is that a hierarchy is a system of Chinese box-like substructures each subsumed and subsuming other similarly organized "boxes." In contradistinction to this, as noted by Simon (1969) and later Duvall (1975), is the usage that implies that there is simply an organizing principle based upon authority relations which parses elements of the system into mutually exclusive subsets. It is this latter meaning which is intended herein. Thus, for our purposes, a hierarchy is simply a set of elements that is organized into subsets of elements *via* ranks. A hierarchical system is one in which the organization is based upon characteristics of the set of relations among elements.

The notion of hierarchy, therefore, contains four assumptions. First, it presumes the existence of some system of organization which links together elements. Second, it implies that this system is organized into recognizable subsystems which themselves are ordered or organized into ranks. Third, these subsets and ranks are viewed as mutually exclusive, so that elements in one subset at a given rank do not belong to another subset at a different or similar rank. Finally, the notion of hierarchy assumes that the ordering of subsets is related to a principle which itself is based upon authority relations. Summarizing, hierarchy refers to the organization of subsets of elements in a system into mutually exclusive strata which are ordered by the principle of sub- and superordination. Simon notes:

> Etymologically the word "hierarchy" ... has generally been used to refer to a complex system in which each of the subsystems is subordinated by authority relations to the system it belongs to. More exactly, in a hierarchic *formal* organization, each system consists of a "boss" and a set of subordinate subsystems. Each of the subsystems has a "boss" who is the immediate subordinate of the boss of the system [1967:87; emphasis added].

It should be carefully noted that Simon further extends the definition to include hierarchies which are not "formal" in the sense used above.

Hierarchical position then, simply refers to the level within a hierarchic system held by an element or set of elements. Thus, units at the higher levels in the hierarchy have fewer subsets of elements to which they are "subordinated." Elements at the lower levels in the hierarchy are subordinated to a multitude of subsets of elements which are themselves higher in the ordering scheme.

Many representational schemes exist to illustrate what is meant by hierarchy; most notable among them is perhaps the graph theoretic approach of Harary and Miller (1970). The graph theoretic representation will be avoided here for reasons of simplicity. Suffice it to say that the approach involves looking at the pattern of relationships among all elements of an interaction (adjacency) matrix. Simon has implicitly included such an approach when he notes:

[122]

If we make a chart of social interactions, of who talks to whom, the clusters of dense interaction in the chart will identify a rather well-defined hierarchic structure. The groupings in this structure may be defined operationally by some measure of frequency of interaction in this sociometric matrix [1969:88].

Thus, it is here argued that a hierarchically organized system itself embeds propositions about the hierarchical position of each of the subsets of elements within that system. Similarly, the notion of hierarchy implies certain "rules" for the interaction among all of the elements within that system. One obvious example is seen by briefly examining a hierarchically organized formal organization (i.e., an institution), such as an international organization. Those elements within the top level in the hierarchy, for example the secretariat, have direct interaction only with a substrata of undersecretariats, each of which is in turn responsible for interaction with the employees within a certain division of the organizational structure. Thus, one obvious rule of interaction in such a system is that direct interaction between any two elements or subsets thereof can either occur at the same aggregate level in the hierarchy or it can at most traverse one level. However, it must be stressed that all hierarchies are not organized as simply as the one described here. A differently organized hierarchy would of course have different implications for the nature of the interaction patterns among elements. The exact type of implications (rules) is, in fact, determined by the structure of the existing system. Researchers (Brams, 1966; Hart, 1974) have attempted to stand this relationship on its head by inferring the type of systemic organization, i.e., the type of hierarchy, by examining the interaction patterns, as originally suggested by Simon. This powerful possibility suggests that the interaction patterns will not only reveal "something" about the structure of the system, but that once the structure of the system is known, it is possible to glean new information from the original interaction patterns.

Finally in terms of definitions, a hierarchy is a self-monitoring structure in that (1) it remains relatively stable over time, and (2) has mechanisms built into it which are regenerative. The implications of these two parts of the definition of structure are relatively easy to draw out; however, they are crucially important. The first notion is that a structure is a relatively stable pattern of relationships, i.e., does not change appreciably over time, among elements in a system. This, of course, implies the existence of a subsystem, which is tautological in that the discussion began with the notion of hierarchical systems.

More important than the constancy of interaction patterns is the reason for such invariance; the lack of change is primarily the direct result of the rules of interaction. To that extent, the structure is stable, because the rules of interaction in part preclude a change in the overall patterns of interactions. Secondly, a structure is stable over time because it dynamically regenerates itself. That is, the individual interactions are constrained by the rules to be reinforcing of the boundaries of the structure. In terms of the institutional example given above, an individual board member may be removed from the system, but the system will reproduce (reintroduce) a new element (individual) for that position, and furthermore that individual will be constrained by the same sets of rules of interaction as were previous members. Moreover, aside from the replacement of individual elements within a system, regeneration also implies that when additional elements are joined with the existing system, they will be incorporated in a manner which is similar to the existing mode of organization. Thus, the influx of new, additional elements will not result in a change in any of the rules of interaction, nor in the regenerative mechanism itself. In summary, the structure notion as presented here extends beyond the Parsonian perspective of patterned interaction to include the notion of why patterns of interaction are stable over time.

The explication of the terms "hierarchical position," "hierarchical interaction," and "structure monitoring" has been undertaken with little if any explicit reference to the system for which they are obviously intended in this study—the international system. The reason for this is straightforward since it is argued that the type of hierarchy which does exist among the elements of a system determines the relative forms which each of these components may take. It is asserted herein that the contemporary international system is hierarchically organized. It can be readily seen that the structure of an international system is directly related to the international distribution of resources and interactions among elements within that system. The following section will explore the relationship of these terms to the contemporary international system via a set of theoretical statements from which testable propositions will be derived. Thus, the original research question resurfaces: How is the international distribution of goods and values related to the internal distribution of goods and values?

5.3 TOWARD A THEORY OF EXTERNAL AND INTERNAL EQUALITY

This section attempts to utilize the concepts developed above, which define hierarchies, in an axiomatic framework, allowing deductions about the relationships between the international external distribution of goods. What follows draws fundamentally upon the work of Norwegian sociologist Johan Galtung (1971), among others, for a definition of the exact type of hierarchical system which is pertinent for the description of the international system of the 120 contemporary polities studied herein (*circa* 1970). It also borrows certain causal descriptions from the aforementioned work of Baumgartner, Buckley, and Burns (1975a).

Even with the rather explicit definitional framework of what comprises a hierarchical system as given above, it is necessary by one means or another to determine the exact form of the hierarchy before one can reinterpret the dyadic relationships of the elements within the system or before it is ultimately possible to relate the behavior within the structure to the structure itself. One plausible, and fruitful, way of accomplishing this would be to study the interaction patterns among the 120 polities. It would be beneficial to study their dyadic interactions over a moderate period of time, from five to ten years, on a number of relevant dimensions of behavior such as conflict, cooperation, and coordination. Thus, one might look at the dyadic trade, aid, tourism, communication, and alliance matrices, among many others, over the last ten years. Appropriately interpreted, it would be possible to determine if there is a hierarchical system of interaction and, if so, exactly what type of hierarchy it is. Whether a hierarchy exists and, if so, what type are both empirical as well as theoretical questions. Unfortunately, they comprise a very large and complex question which cannot be fully addressed within this study. Fortunately however, parts of this question have received some prior attention by scholars, and that attention will be examined and utilized herein.

Johan Galtung's (1971) pioneering article "A Structural Theory of Imperialism" contains many ideas about the mechanisms and types of

FIGURE 5.1. Feudal Hierarchy Adapted from Galtung (1971)

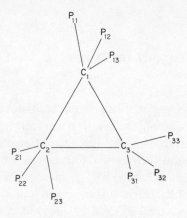

interaction among contemporary elements in the international system. Perhaps the most useful of these ideas for the present effort is that of a feudal, center-periphery structure. This notion mirrors the more traditional scholar's and journalist's notions of a polarized world dominated by a small number of superpowers. Basically, Galtung divides the world into two classes of nations: the center (C) nations and those on the periphery of the world interaction structures (P). Four rules determine the type of interaction possible within this feudal structure:

(1) interaction between Center and Periphery is vertical
(2) interaction between Periphery and Periphery is missing
(3) multilateral interaction involving all three is missing
(4) interaction with the outside world is monopolized by the Center, with two implications:
    (a) Periphery interaction with other Center nations is missing
    (b) Center as well as Periphery interaction with Periphery nations belonging to other Center nations is missing [1971:89].

An interaction structure implied by these rules is adapted from Galtung and shown in Figure 5.1. Galtung calls this the "if you stay off my satellites, I will stay off yours" feudal system (1971:89). Several components of this system are readily interpreted via the earlier discussion of hierarchy. First, one will note that in major ways the system Galtung depicts is identical to the diagram of a hierarchical formal organization. Essentially, there are only two levels or tiers within this hierarchy: the center nations are at one level and the periphery nations at the other. Communication between any two elements in the system must "pass through," or be conducted with, at least one of the center nations. Thus, peripheral elements do not interact directly with other peripheral elements. This holds even for the peripheries of similar center elements.

Research which in one form or another addresses the accuracy of such a portrayal of the interaction patterns among elements in the international system has not been overwhelming in quantity—but neither has it been totally neglected. The work of Steven Brams (1966) represents one of the first attempts to look at the hierarchical nature of transaction matrices among elements in the international system. Through a variety of clustering techniques he was able to "decompose" the members of the international system into several distinct overlapping and non-overlapping subsets. One of the conclusions which he drew from his study was that "the Communist nations form quite private subgroups on all the maps (of transaction matrices) ... (but) ... it appears that diplomatic and economic penetration of the Communist world are more easily achieved than penetration through institutional arrangements... (p. 889)." Skjelsbaek (1969) has studied the IGO and NGO memberships of contemporary polities and has found that there is a marked concentration in the patterns of memberships of nations to such organizations. That is, quite expectedly, some nations appear to be nodes of communication and interaction among all the elements within the system. Russett (1967) has studied the clustering of nations among several dimensions, behavioral and structural, and has found that the dimensions of economic development, agricultural intensity, size, catholic culture, and communism are the most salient in differentiating homogeneous groups of nations. These studies tend to suggest the existence of various types of hierarchies of interactions and characteristics among contemporary political actors in the international system. Indeed, in various forms they suggest the importance of the communist *versus* non-communist status of polities in determining within which cluster any given nation may fall.

More directly related to the question of feudalism is the work of Alger and Hoovler (1974) as well as Modelski (1973). Each of these studies, in a different manner, attempts to directly address the question of feudal interaction patterns. Alger and Hoovler looked at the number of co-memberships in international governments (IGO) and non-governmental organizations (INGO). They found the existence of a

Galtung-type structure in which there were three basic center elements: North America, Western Europe, and Eastern Europe. The conclusion which may be drawn from their study is that "periphery" nations do not, for the most part, interact with other periphery nations except through contacts which are mutually shared with a center nation. Modelski (1973) has studied the actual inter-elite communication and interaction at international organizaions in 1965 and found similar results.

Following Harary (1953-4) and Harary and Miller (1970), Jeffrey Hart (1974) has illustrated the potential of di-graph analysis of trees and lattices for understanding the "structure" of international systems. With enough data, time, and insight it should be possible to address this question more directly in the future. For the present however, with what impressions do the above type of studies leave us?

It is not possible to be absolutely certain of the answer to an empirical question upon such fragmentary evidence, but the extant evidence is not without merit and considerable potential. It seems apparent from most accounts that the international system is not randomly organized: interactions seem to follow patterns, both over time and other dimensions, such as cooperation and conflict. Moreover, based on prior studies it seems reasonable to assert that a selected subset of nations, typically associated with the Soviet and American blocs, are central nations in the sense that their presence in most every sort of interaction is pervasive. The influence of the United States and several Western European nations is by many accounts the most potent, but the influence of the Soviet Union is both potent and perhaps more consistent across different dimensions.

Since 1970, there have been several international events which have potentially modified this picture. The emergence of *détente* could perhaps be argued as either destructive or reinforcing of the feudal characteristics of the posited hierarchy. One thing is clear however: policies such as those resulting in the Berlin Accords of 1971 and *Ostpolitic,* in general, have tended to somewhat loosen up the rigidity of non-peripheral interaction across the two major blocs. Certainly, the "awakening" of the Third World nations both within and without institutional contexts such as the United Nations signifies a new challenge to this hierarchical structure. The "oil-crisis" certainly was one manifestation which was perceived as threatening to the extant international order (Tucker, 1975). However, in spite of these more recent events, it is asserted here that based upon the empirical evidence that does exist, a Galtung-like characterization of the international hierarchy of the 1970 period seems not only plausible but reasonable.

If the definitions of the components of hierarchy are verisimilitudinous and if the assertion that a feudal hierarchy is pertinent for understanding the interactions of the sample of 120 contemporary polities is not grossly inaccurate, what can be deduced about the relationships between external and internal equality? Without additional assumptions, very little. It is to these further assumptions that attention must now be focused.

Three assumptions are posited which relate information about the goal-seeking orientation of all of the elements within the system. First, it is assumed that given a feudal hierarchy as described above, the higher the hierarchical position of any element in the system, the more value will be attached to the stability of the hierarchy by that element (A5.1G). This simply assumes that those elements which are at nodes high in the hierarchy will value stability in direct relation to their level in the hierarchy; it does not assume, it should be emphasized, that lower elements will necessarily value instability of the hierarchy.

Second, in the presence of a feudal hierarchy, all elements in the system will seek to maximize their individual positions within the hierarchy (A5.2G). There are two immediate implications of this assumption which must be explored in order to justify its inclusion. If hierarchies tend overall to be stable feudal structures, as assumed above, then it should be true that they are also relatively static. Further, if these feudal hierarchies are essentially two-level hierarchies, in what sense do individual elements "seek to maximize" their individual positions? First, they may seek to keep their relative position in the hierarchy. More importantly however, they seek to maximize their positions within any *given* level of the hierarchy. This explicitly assumes that within each subset of elements, i.e., the peripheral nations, individual elements are ordered by the intensity of their interaction with elements at higher levels in the hierarchy, $C1$. Thus, the intensity of hierarchical interaction relates directly to the goal seeking maxim. Reexamining Figure 5.1, a visual interpretation becomes apparent. Consider the lengths of the arrows between any center set of elements, e.g., $C1$, and its peripheral elements, $P11$, $P12$, and $P13$. If the length indicates the intensity of hierarchical interaction with shorter lengths representing greater intensity, then it is seen that individual elements within a given level may have different degrees of interaction with higher levels. It is this intensity of hierarchical interaction which elements seek to maximize. It is possible for a "revolutionary" element to desire to change the system rather than merely improve its position within the existing one.

The third assumption about the goal-related behavior of polities within the political hierarchy is that the elements will each attempt to maximize their individual resources (of relevance) within the system (A5.3G). Again, one disclaimer must be interjected: this assumption does not directly imply, in conjunction with A5.2G, that a conflict is built into the system. That is, neither joint-maximization nor collective maximization is necessarily invalidated by this assumption.

In the presence of the goal seeking assumptions, the following axioms are posited:

(A5.6) The posession of relevant resources (RR) and the existence of hierarchical interaction (HI) determine the position (HL) of any element within the hierarchy.

$$RR \cdot HI \rightarrow HL$$

(A5.7) The position of any element within the given hierarchy determines the possession of meta-resources (MR).

$$HI \rightarrow MR$$

The introduction of a new term, meta-resources, is apparent. What is meant by this term is borrowed from Baumgartner and Burns (1974):

Differential control over resources and position in a structure of international relations gives differential meta-power, that is, differential opportunities to structure ... to their benefit and the benefit of their national actors the institutions and rules governing international economic exchange ... (1974:3).

The term meta-power is equated with the possession of meta-resources, except that no constraint is put upon the exchange: exchanges may be economic or non-economic. Meta-resources include (1) mechanisms for influencing the relative level of the resources of others in the hierarchy (RM) and (2) mechanisms for influencing the maintenance of the absolute position of other elements within the hierarchy (LM). Thus;

$$MR = df (RM \cdot LM)$$

[130]

A third axiom is given as follows:

(A5.8) The possession of meta-resources implies their usage (U).

$$MR \rightarrow UMR$$

Usage is implied in the sense that the possession of meta-resources, at a minimum, constrains the possession of meta-resources by other elements and subsets of elements within the hierarchy. Again, this does not preclude the possibility of alliances and coalitions which may be based upon collective goods.

Several important deductions follow from the previous axioms. First, it is shown that the possession of relevant resources and the existence of hierarchical interactions implies the possession of meta-resources (combining A5.6 and A5.7):

(D5.1) $RR \cdot HI \rightarrow MR$ and (UMR)

Further, the total set of distinct elements within the system (T) is decomposable by reference to the hierarchical level into two subsets: one (X) which possesses, to a greater extent, a high degree of meta-resources and one which does not (Y):

(D5.2) $MR_t = df (RMx \cdot LMx) \cdot (RMy \cdot LMy)$

such that $RMx \cdot LMx > RMy \cdot LMy$

This follows from the assumption that the given hierarchy is a feudal one. Moreover, if we posit the existence of a prior positive change in the total resources available within the system, RT, the change in the meta-resources of those elements at the higher levels in the hierarchy (X), should be greater than the change in the meta-resources of those lower in the hierarchy (Y):

(D5.3) $\Delta MR_t \rightarrow \Delta MR_x > \Delta MR_y$

This differential change of resources as a portion of system resources is now defined as the efficiency of adsorption (EA) of new resources. Additionally, it is noted that the efficiency of adsorption is thereby directly related to the level in the hierarchy. The greater the hierarchical position, given the existence of some prior growth in the total

[131]

resources available for distribution throughout the system, the greater the efficiency of adsorption of new resources:

(D5.4) HL→EA

The level of adsorptive efficiency which is possessed by elements within a feudal hierarchy depends upon virtually all of the components of the framework which are unfolded here. The possession of the regenerative meta-resources, the intensity of the hierarchical interactions, the actual level of relevant resources, and the hierarchical position each in their own way as well as collectively, "affect" the adsorptive efficiency (EA) of every element within the hierarchy. This has important implications for the study of inequality. Both types of meta-resources, RM and LM, are each characteristics which refer not only to the individual elements in the system but more precisely they are characteristics of the set of elements within the systemic *milieu*. As such, at a bare minimum, they constrain the inner workings of each element within that system. From the perspective of the model of the domestic determinants of inequality (II) which was posited and examined empirically previously, it is postulated that in several ways the international factors explicated here are themselves related to the level of inequality which is present within each polity.

These external factors are directly related to inequality inasmuch as the adsorptive efficiency itself pertains to the internal as well as external characteristics of a polity. First, it should be apparent from the above arguments that the position in the hierarchy and the possession of relevant resources are interrelated. Since resources which are distributed internally within the polity, such as economic and social product, are among the resources which are relevant, it definitionally follows that the international components are indirectly related to the internal components of the model which seeks to explain inequality via the level of resources among other internal variables. In the form of economic and social productivity, resources have been shown to be centrally important in theoretically and empirically explaining differences in the level of internal inequality across contemporary polities. If the international factors constrain the resources, and the resources in turn constrain the level of inequality, then the international factors themselves constrain the level of inequality:

(D5.5) EF→II

Additionally, it is assumed that the (1) intensity of hierarchical interaction and (2) the possession, and (3) the usage of meta-resources are directly related to the possession of relevant resources (A5.9). This linkage further underscores the interrelated nature of the internal and external components of the theoretical perspective. It follows from this that the hierarchical interaction and possession and usage of meta-resources are related to the level of inequality within polities:

(A5.9) $MR \cdot HI \rightarrow RR$

(D5.6) $HI \rightarrow II$

(D5.7) $MR \rightarrow II$

These external factors are related to inequality not only because they constrain the level of resources as is drawn in deductions (D5.6) and (D5.7), but also because the adsorptive efficiency itself is relevant to the internal as well as external characteristics of a polity.

Simply, meta-resources can be used internally as well as externally. For example, consider a large multinational financial institution. This is one manifestation of a meta-resource that may allow a very efficient adsorption of resources from elements which are lower in the hierarchy, in the sense that the MNC itself has structured interactions and rules as to extract a great deal of value from its interactions with the other elements. The mere fact that it will grant loans, for example, to lower elements and garner interest on the repayment of such loans is but one indication. Perhaps more illustrative is the fact that resources, specifically capital, from elements low in the hierarchy—e.g., Third World polities—will by necessity be placed at the disposal of the bank in question. In addition to this cross-level efficiency such a bank might provide, it also is an institution which is powerful at a given level within the hierarchy: the people and organizations at the same level can also utilize the efficiencies and meta-resources of the institution in internal matters, such as might for example result in higher levels of productivity. Furthermore, the existence of such mechanisms tends to result in increased intensity of hierarchical interaction. The hierarchical interaction itself can lead to increases in the level of inequality not only by restraining the level of resources but by influencing the type of resources which may flow from elements lower in the hierarchy to those that are higher. Succinctly, the flow of resrouces to high elements may well conform to the principle of greater efficiency. That is, they will be resources that can most easily be reconverted into new resources. The flow of resources downward in the hierarchy will tend to be of resources which are difficult to reconvert.

From this it follows that one might simply expect the domestic model to operate more accurately in polities at higher levels within the hierarchy, that possess more meta-resources, and have higher levels of interactions along hierarchical lines.

In the previous section, hierarchy was defined in terms of three components: (1) hierarchical position, (2) hierarchical interaction, and (3) system monitoring. This section has related these components of hierarchy to a series of assumptions about behavior and structure that are viewed as relevant for understanding the contemporary international system. In addition to positing certain interrelationships among these components of hierarchy and the assumptions, several deductions were drawn, some of which related the internal and external distribution of goods within the international system. Since in seeking explicitness the thread of the argument has become rather long, it may prove useful to summarize it in substantive terms and to relate that summary to the more general form of the argument as presented in the definitions, assumptions, and deductions.

It has been shown, based upon prior theoretical and empirical work, that a two-tiered, feudal hierarchy is relevant for describing the international system of the 1960s and early 1970s. This system is one in which a few superpowers, namely the Soviet Union and the United States, have dominated the interaction patterns of virtually all of the other elements within the system. National units, i.e., polities, have often been characterized as goal-seeking structures that attempt to maximize national power (Morgenthau, 1956). More explicitly, it is assumed here that those polities which are higher in the feudal hierarchy will tend to value the stability of the hierarchy since they derive the most benefit from its structure (A5.1G). Within any given tier, polities may be ranked with respect to how intensely they interact with polities higher in the hierarchy. The intensity of this interaction along the line of the given hierarchical structure represents another property, which is related to the goals of individual polities. It is assumed that polities will seek to maximize their interaction with those higher in the structure. Thus, recognizing the structure that does exist, it is assumed that within any tier, polities will seek to maximize their hierarchical interactions and to minimize their nonhierarchical interactions (A5.2G). Finally, the simple assumption is made that polities desire to maximize their resources (A5.3G).

It is further posited that the hierarchical position of any element is at least partially determined by the extent to which that element possesses resources and the extent to which its interaction follows hierarchical lines (A5.6). Axiom (5.7) states that the meta-resources by which elements may structure their interactions with others are possessed in relation to the hierarchical position occupied by that element. That is, the higher in the hierarchy, the more numerous the meta-resources the element will possess (A5.7). Further, it is assumed that the possession of meta-resources implies their usage (A5.8). Succinctly, these assumptions posit that a polity will be positioned at higher levels within the hierarchy if it possesses resources and "obeys" the rules of interaction. The higher in the hierarchy, the more likely the possession of meta-resources which are then used to structure interactions.

From this it is deduced that if a feudal hierarchy exists (D5.1), a polity which has resources and hierarchical interaction will also have meta-resources. The next series of deductions aims at showing that polities with large amounts of meta-resources will be more efficient in adsorbing whatever new resources may be generated within a system (D5.2 through 5.4). This is true because not only do they possess resources, but these resources may be used externally and internally within any given polity. Finally, it is shown that these external mechanisms which deal with the structure of an international system, and thereby constrain the behaviors of its members, are also related to the level of inequality within individual polities. This occurs in two basic ways: (1) the general level of resources are affected by the extent of hierarchical interaction and the possession of meta-resources by some elements in the system to the exclusion of others, and (2) hierarchical interaction and the use of meta-resources themselves effect the inequality by transferring products out of some elements and into others. In the first way, the structure directly effects inequality by constraining the amount of resources, and in the second way it indirectly effects inequality. This general argument is schematically shown in Figure 5.2.

5.4 SPECIFICATION AND OPERATIONALIZATION

As with the previous model of the solely internal determinants of inequality, it is now necessary to turn to the operationalization of (1) the theory in terms of mathematically exact statements of the relation-

FIGURE 5.2. A Schematic Presentation of the Linkages between the Hierarchical Components and Inequality

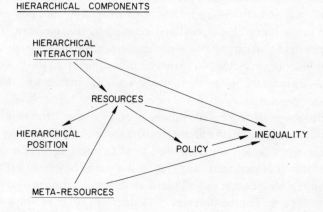

ships entailed, and (2) the variables used in these statements. Even the relatively precise argument presented above and shown in Figure 5.2 must be further refined before any rigorous empirical examination can occur. Both the operationalization of variables and the mathematical specification of the interrelationships among these variables must not only be undertaken, but must be accomplished in a manner which preserves the fabric of the argument developed. The measurement of the primary dependent variable, inequality, was examined in great detail in Chapter Two. Chapters Three and Four detailed the operationalization of the internal variables and development as well as tests of the linkages among these variables and inequality. What remains are the external variables and their linkages. Seven equations have been developed which utilize five new, international variables, as well as several multiplicative interaction terms. These equations will be dealt with sequentially; the variables and operationalizations will be discussed as they are introduced.

$$(5.1) \quad X1 = \alpha + \beta_{11}X10 \cdot X11 + \beta_{12}X10 \cdot X12$$

Specification This equation relates the definitional components of hierarchy to the level of resources available to the polity. It has been argued that hierarchical interaction and meta-resources both have direct links to the level of resources which a polity possesses. Defini-

[136]

tionally, each of the components is interrelated. Since these linkages are definitional rather than causal, they will not be analyzed here. However, it is argued that hierarchical position (X10) interacts in a multiplicative fashion with both hierarchical interaction (X11) and meta-resources (X12). Each interaction term (X10·X11 and X10·X12) is further argued to have a positive impact upon the amount of resources available within the polity; thus, $\beta 11$ and $\beta 12$ are each positive.

Operationalization: **X1** The level of resources available within the polity is measured by the *per capita* energy consumption of metric tons of coal equivalents (ENGCON). This variable is essentially equated with the level of development as suggested by the theory. It does not, of course, tap all of the components of usable resources, but rather is an aggregate summary of them.

X10 As suggested before, the determination of hierarchical position is problematic in that it presumes prior knowledge of the hierarchical structure. Given the fact that a feudal hierarchy has been posited, it is assumed that the higher elements will have more total interaction and communication with other elements. This is true because those high in the feudal hierarchy tend to interact with most all of the lower elements, whereas the low elements tend only to interact with a few higher elements. Since diplomatic interaction is one important component of internation communication, and since data are readily available on this measure, the number of embassies which a polity maintains in other nations is used to construct a variable which may serve as the surrogate for hierarchical position. The exact formulation was to use the percentage of the systemic total number of embassies held by any individual polity (HRRCHY). Thus, polities with a large percentage of the total number of embassies in the system are viewed as being higher in the hierarchy than polities with a small percentage. It must be noted that one plausible interpretation of the actual score which an individual nation receives on this variable is that large nations will receive high scores, and small nations will get low scores. In fact, there is some correlation, but it is not large. Economic size, as measured by Gross National Product, is correlated 0.38. The correlation of both X10 and geographic size with total population is also relatively small (about 0.20 in each instance). Thus, it is assumed that the artifact due solely to size is not overwhelming.

[137]

X11 Hierarchical interaction is measured by the intensity of trade. Specifically, the percentage of imports from either of these nations was added to the percentage of exports to either of them. The measure thus created (SUPTRD) is greater for those countries which have a high concentration of trade with the highest elements in the hierarchy.

X12 Possession of meta-resources can only be measured very imperfectly. Much substantive literature suggests the multinational corporation (MNC) may be a very powerful extractive resource. The number of multinational corporations operating within any polity is taken as the operationalization of this variable. It will be seen that elements both high and low in the hierarchy may well have a high score on this variable. An important distinction is whether the MNCs are based or operating within individual polities. Further, it is often true that elements lower in the hierarchy have only a few MNCs operating within them. These two reasons suggest why the interaction of this term with the hierarchical position (X10) is so important. Polities high in the hierarchy with a large number of MNCs possess a large number of meta-resources, while elements low in the hierarchy with a large number of MNCs have fewer meta-resources.

(5.2) $X4 = \alpha + \beta_{21}X1$

Specification Previously explored in Chapter Four, this equation states that the more developed a polity, the more extensive will be its educational policy (X4); thus, $\beta21$ is greater than zero.

Operationalization: **X4** The number of universities within a polity is used (UNVRSTY).

(5.3) $X4 = \alpha + \beta_{31}X1$

Specification In a similar fashion, highly developed polities tend to have an extensive set of institutional programs dealing with unemployment. The factor score of the social security program analysis is used (UNEMFAC). $\beta31$ is positive.

(5.4) $X10 = \alpha + \beta_{41}X1$

Specification This equation is related to equation (5.1) in that they each concern the causes and consequences of hierarchical position.

The equation specifies that hierarchical position is in part a reflection of the level of internal resources possessed by a polity. The indirect, simultaneous feedback between equations (5.1) and (5.4) will be discussed in the following section on estimation and evaluation.

(5.5) $X13 = \alpha + \beta_{51}(X10-k)^{\frac{1}{2}}$

Specification This equation suggests that the type of hierarchical interaction (X13) is a function of hierarchical position. The exact function was initially presumed to be linear, but an examination of the scattergram showed clear curvilinearity and the above square-root transformation captures that form. The substantive meaning is explored briefly in the discussion of operationalization.

Operationalization: **X13** This measure of extractive hierarchical interaction is the Galtung-Hongro Trade Composition Index (GALTUNG). The initial definition was proposed in Galtung (1971:101ff). It is calculated:

$$X13 = \frac{(a + d) - (b + c)}{(a + b + c + d)}, \text{ where}$$

a = raw imports
b = raw exports
c = manufactured imports and
d = manufactured exports

Galtung refers to this as the "vertical trade" variable (1971:101). The imports of nations with a high positive score, such as Japan, are overwhelmingly raw materials, while their exports are almost entirely manfactured goods. A large negative score indicates export of raw materials and imports consisting of manufactured goods. Nations with near-zero scores have a "balanced" trade picture in that they tend to export and import both raw materials and processed goods. "Raw" and "manufactured" goods were defined with respect to the Standard International Trade Classifications (SITC): commodities in SITC categories below 7 were defined as raw, while the rest were considered to be manufactured (SITC = 7, 8, and 9).

Figure 5.3 shows the scattergram of X10 and X13. It suggests that there is a set of polities which have low hierarchical position but are very extractive in their trade relations. From that extreme, the impact of hierarchical position upon X13 declines steadily to a minimum

FIGURE 5.3. Scatterplot of Hierarchical Position (X10) and the Galtung-Hongro Trade Composition Index (X13)

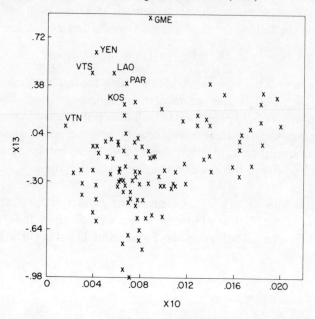

(.00715), and then changes slope and increases steadily. The polities which are low in the hierarchy but have highly extractive trade interactions tend to be satellite-type countries under the strong military domination of a major power. Also they have a high level of indigenous conflict. Five of the outstanding examples are shown in Figure 5.3: Yemen, North and South Vietnam, South Korea, and Laos. It is interesting to note that not only is indigenous conflict present in most of these polities, but external military penetration is evident in many of them as well. For all intents and purposes, each of these polities is "tied" by a strong and active alliance to a major power which is high in the hierarchy—and which also is extractive in its own trade relations. This curvilinear influence will be approximated by the addition of a constant, k, to X10, and by taking the square root of the result.

(5.6) $X14 = \alpha + \beta_{61}X10$

Specification   The hierarchical position is argued to increase the degree of trade:structure reproduction (X14) possessed by any nation. Because of the scoring of this index, $\beta 61$ is negative.

Operationalization: **X14** This variable measures the "diversification" of trade. Specifically, it is the extent to which a nation's trade pattern, across commodities and partners, is homomorphic to the general or average pattern which best summarizes global trade interaction. Thus, the measure assesses the absolute deviation of the country's commodity shares from the world structure:

$$X14 = \sum_{i}^{N} |h_{ij} - h_i|/2, \text{ where}$$

h_{ij} = the share of commodity i in the total exports of country j
h_i = the share of commodity i in total world trade

A country has a low score on this index if its trade is a complete "mirror" of the world trade structure; a high score represents an imperfect or incomplete reflection of the world trade structure by an individual nation's trade picture.

$$(5.7) \quad Y = \alpha + \beta_{71}X2 + \beta_{72}X2 \cdot X3$$
$$+ \beta_{73}X4 + \beta_{74}X5 + \beta_{75}X10 \cdot X12$$
$$+ \beta_{76}X13 + \beta_{77}X14$$

Specification The first four terms, from X2 to X5, are taken from Chapters Three and Four, and represent the internal determinants of inequality. Rapid growth (X2) aggravates inequality—i.e., $\beta71$ is positive—while each of the other internal variables, from structurally diversified growth (X2·X3), to educational (X4) and unemployment (X5) policies tend to reduce inequality and therefore have negative coefficients ($\beta72$, $\beta73$, and $\beta74$). The interaction of hierarchical position and MNCs is argued to result directly in greater levels of inequality through the transfer of efficient resources out of the polity: $\beta75$ is negative. The other two terms (X13 and X14) are posited to have opposite effects from one another. The trade composition index, X13, should directly result in lower levels of inequality, since a high score reflects a polity which "exploits" other polities. A high score on X14 indicates a low degree of trade latitude and should be associated with higher levels of inequalities. Thus, $\beta76$ should be positive.

In the next section, the estimation procedures and problems will be detailed. Following that presentation, a substantive evaluation of the "results" will indicate some of the problems and some of the promise of the model and theory.

[141]

5.5 EMPIRICAL EVALUATION

The model developed in equations (5.1) through (5.7) can be sequentially estimated via classical linear regression, since each of the equations is linear and no direct, simultaneous feedback is involved between any two or more equations. However, the model does present several design problems which may influence the estimation and interpretation of results. These questions are, for the most part, themselves interrelated, although the question of the recursiveness of the model will be addressed first.

It has been asserted that there is no direct, simultaneous feedback among these seven equations. Classically, this is true, since no two variables are taken as determinants of each other. There is, however, a certain nonrecursive character to the theoretical argument about the nature of hierarchy. In general, this concerns the systemic monitoring of the hierarchical system via structuring of the rules of interactions. In particular, it has been argued that both hierarchical interaction and meta-resources affect the level of resources available within any polity. In turn, the level of resources which a polity possesses is related to the level it occupies within the hierarchy. Clearly, this is a feedback mechanism in that the nature of the hierarchy structures the resources and interactions of the elements, and the resources possessed by the elements within the hierarchy also structure the hierarchy itself.

While this argument may be intractable in a certain sense, it is by no means inexplicably counterintuitive. The specification of the argument seeks to capture this "nonrecursiveness" without totally invalidating the ordinary least-squares approach. Since the covariation among the components of hierarchy is definitional, it was not included in the model. However, the interaction of hierarchical position with both meta-resources and hierarchical interaction was viewed as crucial in understanding how the level of resources within a polity were constrained by the hierarchical structure. Thus, equation (5.1) contains two interaction terms ($X10 \cdot X11$ and $X10 \cdot X12$) as the independent variables explaining the level of resources ($X1$). Equation (5.4) explains the hierarchical position ($X10$) by the level of resources ($X1$). In this manner, the nonrecursive nature of the argument is preserved, but no direct feedback occurs; rather, the feedback is contained within the interaction terms. This representation is consistent with the theoretical argument and does not invalidate the statistical integrity of the equation set in terms of OLS estimation procedures.

Such a solution is both acceptable from a technical standpoint and theoretically understandable. Yet, the reason one is concerned about simultaneous feedback, in the first place, and therefore simultaneous estimation, is that it implies that the error terms from one equation are translated to other equations within the model. This leads to inconsistent and biased estimates of the parameters. Thus, one check does exist on whether the feedback leads to inconsistent estimates: Are the error terms of equations (5.1) and (5.4) highly correlated? To the extent that they are, there is possible bias in the estimates of the parameters derived from OLS estimation.

If such error covariation is uncovered, two solutions are possible: (1) additional variables (exogenous and lagged-endogenous) may be added to the model which will link up to one or both of the feedback variables, thus allowing identification of the equations and a two-stage, or if appropriate, three-stage least squares estimation, and (2) deletion of one or both of the links in question. The first solution requires additional theoretical work, while the second discards theoretical work already undertaken. The error correlation between equations (5.1) and (5.4) is -0.37 (see Table 5.4 below). This implies that less than ten percent of error variance is shared between these two equations. While this is not overwhelming, it is sufficiently large to call the consistency and bias of the estimates into question. Thus, the linkages in equation (5.1) are reported but not emphasized. They should be taken as rough indicators of the causal impact rather than precise coefficients.

The second potential design artifact is the inclusion of independent variables which are multiplicative transformations of other independent variables. Multiplicative terms are problematic in two primary ways. First, if one is using a path analytic strategy, the indirect paths are difficult to assess without computer simulation techniques. Second, the inclusion of multiplicative terms as well as the original variables, for example $X2 \cdot X3$ and $X2$, within a single equation introduces the statistical problem of multicollinearity. As is well established, multicollinearity leads not only to problems of estimation but also to difficulty in interpreting the results. Almost all econometricians recognize that the problem is ultimately intractable. However, there are varying thresholds of multicollinearity which precondition whether or not individual researchers will throw up their hands in despair. One recent suggestion (Rockwell, 1975) has been to test the determinant of the correlation matrix. If the matrix is invertible and has therefore a nonzero determinant, it may be assumed that the problem of multicollinearity does not exist. This interpretation is misleading in the sense that with modern computer algorithms it is possible to invert virtually any matrix which does not have perfect correlation between elements. Somewhat more difficult "tests" have been proposed by Kmenta (1971) and are discussed in Chapter Three. Based upon these guidelines, it has been possible cautiously to reject multicollinearity as a serious problem in the case of the internal variables X2 and X2·X3. The external multiplicative terms are not highly intercorrelated and do not appear in any single equation except equation (5.1), wherein X10·X11 and X10·X12 are correlated 0.30. Thus, it is possible to reject the notion that the multiplicative index construction artificially introduces a high degree of multicollinearity into this particular model.

The final potential design problem to be discussed before proceeding to the data analysis is the question of theory bulldozing. Simply, the concern is with whether conformance to rigorous statistical procedures is appropriate in the case of a relatively novel theoretical model which is virtually untested. By specifying that each coefficient in every equation must not only be significant at the 0.05 level (F-test), but also of the predicted sign, and by requiring that the F-test for the overall equation must also be significantly (0.05) nonzero, is it not possible that the statistical properties of the data will lead to the rejection of propositions advanced here and elsewhere which may be essentially valid? Others have chosen a different path in arguing that the theoretical concerns should outweigh the statistical ones. Such a strategy was rejected here, and only highly significant results, in terms of included variables and accepted equations, are advanced beyond the initial testing procedure. This strategy has the weakness mentioned: it easily allows rejection of theoretically valid propositions for which there are estimation problems, such as multicollinearity. Conversely, however, the results obtained are both statistically and, it is hoped, theoretically significant. Thus, in one sense the rigor allows the theory to be "bulldozed" in cases of weak statistical evidence. Armed with these caveats, discussion now turns to the data analysis.

Table 5.1 presents the results from the OLS estimation of equations (5.1) through (5.7). In general, it shows that the specified model is an accurate representation of the data. Stated differently, the data lend considerable support to the specification of the theory which is proposed. Virtually all of the coefficients are both of the predicted sign and

TABLE 5.1. *Estimation of Full Model of Internal and External Determinants of Inequality in 120 Contemporary Polities as Represented in Equations (5.1) Through (5.7)* [a]

INDEPENDENT VARIABLE	REGRESSION COEFFICIENT	STANDARD ERROR	STANDARDIZED COEFFICIENT
Equation (5.1)	Dependent Variable : X1		
X10X11	.13*	.05	.20
X10X12	.002*	.0002	.58
Equation (5.2)	Dependent Variable : X4		
X1	331.2*	35.28	.66
Equation (5.3)	Dependent Variable : X5		
X1	33.8*	5.8	.48
Equation (5.4)	Dependent Variable : X1		
X10	.14*	.02	.65
Equation (5.5)	Dependent Variable : X13		
$(X10)^{1/2}$	4.5*	1.04	.39
Equation (5.6)	Dependent Variable : X14		
X10	−33.5*	2.49	−.81
Equation (5.7)	Dependent Variable : Y		
X2	2.8*	.78	.53
X2X3	−2.3*	.56	−.57
X4	.001	.006	.02
X5	−.04	.04	−.10
X10X12	.03*	.01	.30
X13	.15	.17	.07
X14	3.49*	.57	.95

Equation	R2	$\overline{R2}$	F	p=	DF[b]
(5.1)	.46	.44	37.8	.000	90
(5.2)	.43	.43	88.2	.000	116
(5.3)	.23	.22	33.8	.000	113
(5.4)	.43	.42	85.4	.000	114

(5.5)	.15	.14	18.8	.000	105
(5.6)	.66	.66	181.1	.000	92
(5.7)	.77	.73	21.2	.000	45

a. Where:

Y	(INEQUAL)	=	Inequality index
X1	(ENGCON)	=	Energy consumption per capita
X2	(IXCONS)	=	Index of short-term economic growth
X3	(DIVERSITY)	=	Index of diversity and infrastructure
X2X3	(INTERACT)	=	Interaction of X2 and X3
X4	(UNVRSTY)	=	Index of educational policy
X5	(UNEMFAC)	=	Index of welfare policy
X10	(HRRCHY)	=	Index of a polities position in the international hierarchy
X11	(SUPTRD)	=	Index of trade interaction with the United States and the Soviet Union
X12	(ALLMNCS)	=	Index of international resources resident within the polity
X10X11		=	Interaction X10X11
X10X12		=	Interaction of X10X12
X13	(GALTUNG)	=	Trade composition of commodity export
X14	(XDVRSTY)	=	Trade diversity score

For extensive definitions, see Appendix B.

b. Significance is based upon the smallest N from the individual correlation matrices. Most coefficients are based on over 100 cases.

* Statistically significant at the 0.05 level or better.

statistically significant. The corrected coefficients of determination, R^2, are generally very robust, and the F-test for each equation is highly significant. The standard error of the estimates is nowhere overwhelmingly disproportionate, and in all but three cases it is at least half the size of the estimated coefficient. Thus, the estimation is very supportive of the theoretical arguments, especially in light of the strictness with which statistical tests have been applied. Each equation is itself, however, worthy of discussion.

The first equation, (5.1), is restated here:

(5.1) $X1 = \alpha + \beta_{51}X10 \cdot X11$

This equation presents the argument that hierarchical interaction and possession of meta-resources each determine the level of resources within a polity, i.e., the level of development. The mechanism through which this occurs is itself an interactive one in which the hierarchical position of a polity is a multiplier of each term. This means that unless accompanied by a relatively high position within the hierarchy, these two variables, meta-resources and hierarchical interaction, will have very little impact themselves upon the level of resources. One way of conceptualizing this interaction is that hierarchical position acts as a gatekeeper of the direct impacts between both meta-resources and hierarchical interaction and the level of internally available resources. In those polities which are high in the hierarchy, the translation of these two independent variables into internal resources is strong; in those polities without a high position in the hierarchy, the translation is weak.

The results from the OLS themselves strongly support this argument. Almost one-half (44 percent) of the cross-national variation in the level of development may be explained by reference to these two interactive variables. Each variable itself has a significant coefficient of the predicted direction. Furthermore, the variance-covariance matrix has no nonzero terms (to two decimals), indicating the absence of heteroscedasticity and multicollinearity. Two motivating factors are elemental in determining the given level of development within a polity: (1) the interaction of hierarchical position and hierarchical interaction patterns, and (2) the interaction of hierarchical position and the possession of meta-resources.

It must be remembered that the exact estimates are somewhat misleading due to error correlation with equation (5.4). Thus, the precise amount of impact is impossible to determine, although the results do suggest that each term has a significant, positive impact upon the level of development. Meta-resources appear to be more strongly associated with the level of internal resources than does hierarchical interaction with the superpowers (standardized coefficients of 0.58 *versus* 0.20).

Both equations, (5.2) and (5.3), represent the policy linkage through which the level of development is seen as generative of policy efforts. In the form of extending education (X4) and unemployment programs (X5), these efforts seek to redistribute societal product to those both within and outside the current work cycle. Each of these linkages is developed and discussed in the previous chapter. The results are merely presented here for completeness.

$$(5.2) \quad X4 = \alpha + \beta_{21}X1$$
$$(5.3) \quad X5 = \alpha + \beta_{31}X1$$

These two equations are each significant in all parameters examined. The $\overline{R2}$ values are strong, respectively 0.42 and 0.23, while the overall F-tests are each significant. The standardized coefficients are both positive and of roughly equal magnitudes, 0.66 and 0.48 respectively.

[147]

Thus, higher levels of development tend to be associated with higher levels of policy effort aimed at reduction of inequalities within the polity.

Equation (5.4) represents part of the monitoring argument:

(5.4) $X10 = \alpha + \beta_{41}X10$

Again, this equation argues that the position occupied by any polity within a feudal hierarchy is in part a function of the level of development within that polity. The data strongly support such a postulation. Roughly forty percent (0.43) of the variance in hierarchical position (X10) is explainable by reference to the level of development within the polity. The standardized regression coefficient (0.48) is both positive and highly significant, as predicted. Substantively, this has two important implications. Not only does the direct link between the hierarchical position and the level of development seem important, but also in conjunction with the results from equation (5.1), the notion of systemic monitoring is upheld. There is an indirect feedback mechanism which will preserve the hierarchical ordering. Relatively well-developed polities will tend to be placed at high levels in the feudal hierarchy. In turn, their possession of meta-resources and high frequencies of interaction along hierarchical lines will, when coupled with hierarchical position, tend to reinforce a high level of development.

In addition to being a multiplier of the impacts between hierarchical interaction and meta-resources, the level a polity holds within a feudal hierarchy itself is a determinant of certain characteristics of a polity's interaction patterns, Specifically, it is postulated that the Galtung-Hongro trade composition index (X13) is a nonlinear function of hierarchical position (X10). The extent to which the export picture of a polity reflects the aggregate structure of world trade (X14) is also determined by hierarchical position. In this case, however, it was predicted that polities at high levels in the hierarchy will have wider latitude in trade relations, and a low score on X14: therefore, the path is predicted to be negative. These bivariate equations have a simple structure:

(5.5) $\quad X13 = \alpha + \beta_{51}(X10)^{\frac{1}{2}}$
(5.6) $\quad X14 = \alpha + \beta_{61}X10$

Each of these two equations has significant coefficients of the appropriate sign and a relatively small standard error. Of all of the estimated equations, (5.5) has the lowest $\overline{R2}$, although the F-test is highly significant. Examination of the scatterplot reveals that there is a rather strong positive association between these two variables, but that a few outliers which have a high score on X13 tend to reduce the variance explained (and probably the estimated regression coefficient). One interpretation is that the nonlinearity could better be approximated by a polynomial rather than the square-root function. This seems likely. More plausible still is the suggestion that the specification of the linkage is theoretically deficient in some aspect in that there seems to be a somewhat different pattern of covariance than was expected between these two variables.

One explanation is that the effects of military penetration and alliance structure are omitted: were countries such as North and South Vietnam, South Korea, Laos, and East Germany excluded, the association would be a strong, positive one. Even more appropriate would be the modeling of the effects of these excluded factors. Thus, there possibly is another intervening or interactive factor which has been left out. Still, the tests indicate a statistically significant relationship in the predicted direction. The impact of hierarchical interaction upon X14 is considerably more distinct. Over sixty-five percent of the variance is explained, the parameters are significant and of the correct sign, and the standardized coefficient is large. In short, each of these equations demonstrates the considerable effect that hierarchical position has upon two aspects of a polity's interaction profiles: in the case of the trade-composition index, the impact is direct and positive, but suggestive of further theoretical work; in the case of trade diversity, the impact is strongly negative.

Equation (5.7) represents the confluence of internal and external factors which impinge upon the level of social inequality within comtemporary polities:

$$(5.7) \quad Y = \alpha + \beta_{71}X2 + \beta_{72}X2 \cdot X3 + \beta_{73}X4 + \beta_{74}X5$$
$$+ \beta_{75}X10 \cdot X12 + \beta_{76}X13 + \beta_{77}X14$$

The first four independent variables are taken from the previously developed work on the internal determinants, i.e., Chapters Three and Four. Concisely, these terms pose the argument that (1) policy efforts which seek to redistribute product tend to reduce inequality ($\beta73$ and $\beta74$ are negative), (2) rapid economic growth tends to aggravate inequality (β71 is positive), and (3) when coupled with a structurally diversified infrastructure, growth will have a dampening impact on inequality (β72 is negative). These arguments were previously examined and considerable support for them was found. The three external links illustrate two primary propositions. First, it is asserted that inequality is decreased by high levels of hierarchical position and meta-resources (β75 is positive). The index of feudalism in trade relations (X13) should reduce inequality (β76 is negative), and the trade latitude index should, *ceteris paribus*, tend to be associated with higher levels of societal inequality (β77 is positive).

The results from the OLS estimation of equation (5.7) are rather mixed. First of all, it is apparent that a great deal of variance is shared between the independent variable set and the dependent variable. Roughly three-quarters of the variance in societal inequality is explained by the linear combination of these seven variables ($\overline{R2}$ = 0.73). However, only four of the seven estimated regression coefficients are significant at the 0.05 level, and some of the coefficients are opposite to the predicted sign.

The impact of economic growth and structurally diversified growth upon inequality remains stable. The pattern uncovered in earlier chapters does not change appreciably. Estimated regression coefficients of these variables are significant, and as predicted, in the opposite sign. Their standard errors are small, and they each have roughly equal magnitudes of impact upon inequality.

The policy variables which were previously found to have strong significant relationships to decreased levels of inequality, have virtually no shared covariance when the international factors are included in the model. Thus, neither X4 nor X5 have significant coefficients, and the estimated, nonsignificant coefficient of X4 (.001) is opposite the sign predicted by the model. This directly contradicts the findings of the estimated, *non*significant coefficient of X4 (.001) is opposite the tional variables.

With respect to the international variables, two of the three relationships are significant and predicted correctly. The relationship between X10·X12 and inequality is significant and positive. Thus, the relative impact of high levels of X10·X12 is to effect higher levels of inequality (the standardized coefficient = 0.30). This significant relationship is opposite what was predicted by the model and theory. Several explanations are plausible, but the upshot of each is simply that when the confluence of internal and external variables are jointly considered, the polities which are both higher in the hierarchy and possess more meta-resources have greater amounts of inequality. Aspects of the multinational corporation, and its use in the index, may shed some light on this problem. It has frequently been argued that MNCs tend to be highly efficient organizations but that their efficiencies do not overlap with the boundaries of the nation state. Thus, the maximization of resources and efficiencies by a MNC may, for example, involve transfer pricing. This will result in the transfer of resources out of some set of countries and into another set. But this transfer may or may not be in line with the hierarchy of polities. The exact direction of such transfers is often highly dependent on economic and political considerations which are undertaken within the organizational context of the MNC. Thus, the linkage is opposite of what was expected, and one highly plausible explanation is because the operational referent of the theory is largely constrained to a nation-centric focus.

Of the variables which have any impact upon societal inequality as measured and specified here, X14 has by far the greatest impact upon inequality. Even when controlling for each of the other six explanatory variables, the covariation between inequality and X14 is large. The coefficient is significant and of the postulated direction. Even more suggestive of the strength of this linkage is the estimated beta coefficient of 0.95. This strongly supports the notion that nations with a low degree of latitude in trade relations, and which therefore do not mirror the aggregate world trade picture, have a much higher level of inequality.

The impression with which one is left after examining Table 5.1 is that equations (5.1) through (5.6) are essentially correct in the sense that the data support the arguments they pose. In equation (5.7), however, it appears that when viewed in the context of both external and internal causes of inequality, some previously supported linkages seem questionable. Specifically, by including the three external variables, the policy linkages do not seem as important as previously thought. In another interpretation, the external variables override the impact of internal policy effort, suggesting the dominance of international variables over domestic ones. Thus, the hierarchical nature of the international system constrains the influence of internal policy variables. It is also possible that the policy variables could drop in significance because of multicollinearity with the external variables.

Since the shared variance between policy indicators and external variables is nowhere greater than forty percent (X14 and X4), this explanation may be dismissed. Furthermore, the impact of X3 is problematic in that, although nonsignificant, it is not in the predicted direction. This implies that when other internal and external variables are included, nations with a large ability to import raw materials and to export processed goods tend to have somewhat higher levels of inequality than the polities that are exploited. This is contrary to the theoretical argument posed above.

In summary, both internal and external variables are important in explaining cross-national differences in the level of inequality. Internally, policy variables do not seem to have much independent impact on levels of societal inequality, whereas the rate of growth alone increased inequality, while structurally diversified growth tends to decrease the level of inequality. With respect to external factors there seem to be two important influences. First, the existence of meta-resources within a polity, even if it is high within the hierarchy, tends to have a significant positive impact upon the level of inequality. The degree to which a nation's trade patterns deviate from the world structure is also significantly related to increased levels of inequality within the polity.

As outlined earlier, equations which contained nonsignificant terms in the initial estimation were respecified and reexamined; since the first six equations were initially upheld, only equation (5.7) needs reexamination. Specifically, the nonsignificant terms were deleted:

$$(5.7^*) \quad Y = \alpha + \beta_{71}X2 + \beta_{72}X2 \cdot X3 + \beta_{73}X10 \cdot X12 + \beta_{74}X14$$

Table 5.2 presents the results of this estimation. With the deletion of the nonsignificant terms, the variance explained does not increase much—still, about three-quarters of the variance in inequality is explained by these four variables. The coefficients are virtually the same as were initially estimated in Table 5.1. This suggests further confirmation of the idea that multicollinearity was not responsible for the nonsignificance of the coefficients X4 and X5. Figure 5.4 presents a schematic diagram of the significant causal relationships depicted by equations (5.1) through (5.6) and (5.7*).

The fact that the linkages between policy variables and inequality drop out when external variables are introduced, raises another in-

TABLE 5.2. *Estimation of Equation (5.7*) Deleting Variables with Non-significant Coefficients in (5.7)* [a]

	Dependent Variable : Y		
INDEPENDENT VARIABLE	REGRESSION COEFFICIENT	STANDARD ERROR	STANDARDIZED COEFFICIENT
X2	3.1*	.74	.59
X2X3	−2.4*	.54	−.60
X10X12	.03*	.01	.31
X14	3.5*	.48	.94

R2	$\overline{R2}$	F	p=	DF[b]
.76	.74	37.4	.000	48

a. All variables as previously defined in Note a, Table 5.1, page 145. For extensive definitions, see Appendix B.
b. Significance is based upon the smallest N from the individual correlation matrix. Most coefficients are based on over 100 cases.
*   Statistically significant at the 0.05 level or better.

teresting question. Specifically, it has been argued that in addition to the links from economic growth and the diversity of the infrastructure to inequality, there is an independent link from the level of development to inequality. Indeed, this is the link with which this investigation was initially begun. Jackman (1975) has argued for the appropriateness of a curvilinear specification of this relationship. The curvilinear forms attempt to approximate the threshold components of various explanations of why, at the high levels of development, there is a diminishing of the impact of the level of development upon reduced inequality. The policy variables were introduced explicitly to specify this argument. Since those linkages drop out when international factors are injected into the explanation, what is implied about the direct relationship between developmental level and inequality? Is the entire effect of development mediated by a polity's level in the hierarchy? Does it appear that international variables completely override the domestic link between the developmental level and the degree of inequality within contemporary polities? Or should the direct link be reestablished?

The latter option may not seem entirely justified, since the data

[153]

FIGURE 5.4. Schematic Representation of the Linkages in the Model of the External and Internal Determinants of Inequality[a]

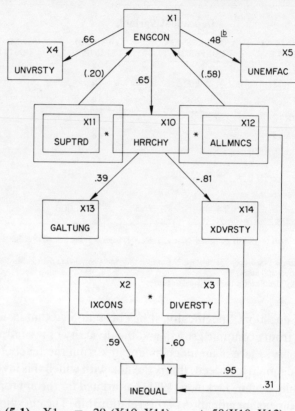

Equation (5.1) $\quad$ X1 $\quad$ = .20 (X10·X11) $\qquad$ +.58(X10·X12)

$\qquad\qquad\qquad$ $\overline{R2}$[c] $\;$ = .44 $\qquad$ F = 37.8 $\qquad$ p ≤ .000

Equation (5.2) $\quad$ X4 $\quad$ = .66(X1)

$\qquad\qquad\qquad$ $\overline{R2}$ = .43 $\qquad$ F = 88.2 $\qquad$ p ≤ .000

Equation (5.3) $\quad$ X5 $\quad$ = .48(X1)

$\qquad\qquad\qquad$ $\overline{R2}$ = .22 $\qquad$ F = 33.8 $\qquad$ p ≤ .000

Equation (5.4) $\quad$ X10 = .65(X1)

$\qquad\qquad\qquad$ $\overline{R2}$ = .42 $\qquad$ F = 85.4 $\qquad$ p ≤ .000

Equation (5.5) $\quad$ X13 = .39(X10)$^{\frac{1}{2}}$

$\qquad\qquad\qquad$ $\overline{R2}$ = .14 $\qquad$ F = 18.8 $\qquad$ p ≤ .000

[154]

FIGURE 5.4. Schematic Representation of the Linkages in the Model of the External and Internal Determinants of Inequality[a] *(cont.)*

Equation (5.6) $X14 = -.81(X10)$

$$\overline{R2} = .66 \qquad F = 181.1 \qquad p \leqslant .000$$

Equation (5.7) $Y = .59(X2) - .60(X2 \cdot X3) + .31(X10 \cdot X12) + .95(X14)$

$$\overline{R2} = .74 \qquad F = 37.4 \qquad p \leqslant .000$$

---

a. Where: INEQUAL (Y) = Composite inequality index
ENGCON (X1) = Energy Consumption per capita
IXCONS (X2) = Index of construction activity
DIVERSTY (X3) = Index of the diversity of the economic infrastructure
UNVRSTY (X4) = Index of Educational policy effort
UNEMFAC (X5) = Index of unemployment policy effort
HRRCHY (X10) = Index of the level which a polity holds within the international feudal hierarchy.
SUPTRD (X11) = Index of trade interaction with the United States and the Soviet Union
ALLMNCS (X12) = Index of international resources resident within the polity
GALTUNG (X13) = Index of trade composition of exports
XDVRSTY (X14) = Index of Trade Latitude

These variables and their components are explained in greater detail in Appendix B wherein reference is made to their introduction into the text.
b. Standardized regression coefficients are reported. For more complete information on estimation, see Tables 5.1 and 5.2. All estimates are statistically significant at the 0.05 level or better.
c. Corrected coefficient of determination is equivalent to the percent of variance in the dependent variable which is explained by the independent variables.
* This symbol represents multiplicative interaction.

analysis allowed a strong rejection of the impact of policy variables on inequality when international factors were excluded. Despite this objection, the question is theoretically meaningful enough to merit at least a cursory empirical examination. The level of development (X1) was reintroduced into equation (5.7*). The resulting equation, the estimation of which is reported in Table 5.3, is extremely telling. The variance explained does not increment significantly, each of the previously estimated coefficients remains of the same sign and roughly same magnitude, and the coefficient for the newly reintroduced development variable is not statistically significant at the 0.05 level—although it is significant at the 0.07 level.

Using the strict 0.05 criterion, one may infer that when internal and external variables are introduced into the prediction equation for inequality, the level of development is found to be unimportant in that explanation. Even if relaxing that criterion slightly, one may fairly say that the level of development has a slight negative impact upon inequal-

TABLE 5.3. *Addition of the Level of Economic Development (X1) to the Estimation of Equation (5.7*)*[a]

	Dependent Variable : Y		
INDEPENDENT VARIABLE	REGRESSION COEFFICIENT	STANDARD ERROR	STANDARDIZED COEFFICIENT
X2	2.56*	.77	.49
X2X3	−2.00*	.57	−.50
X10X12	.03*	.01	.31
X14	2.94*	.55	.80
X1	−6.93	3.73	−.22

R2	$\overline{R2}$	F	p=	DF[b]
.77	.75	32.2	.000	47

a. All variables as previously defined in Note a, Table 5.1, page 145. For extensive definitions, see Appendix B.
b. Significance is based upon the smallest N from the individual correlation matrix. Most coefficients are based on over 100 cases.
* Statistically significant at the 0.05 level or better.

ity, but it does not significantly add to the explanation in the statistical sense. The indirect impact, of course, is still very important.

It was strongly argued above that analyses of residuals should be undertaken in any social science application of least squares methodology. Table 5.4 presents the variance-covariance matrix of the unnormalized regression coefficients. Examination of this matrix lends information about several of the OLS assumptions. Specifically, the variances of the estimated coefficients—i.e., the diagonal elements in the matrix—should be roughly equal. Table 5.3 shows that the variances are relatively small and mostly within the same order of magnitude. However, one variance (X10·X12) is much depressed below the level of the others. This suggests the potential problem of heteroscedasticity. Thus, OLS estimates will be unbiased and consistent, but not efficient. Visual inspection does not reveal any glaring problem in these residuals and the variances themselves are all very small. Thus heteroscedasticity is rejected as a major problem.

Second, the OLS model assumes that the nondiagonal elements in

TABLE 5.4. *Variance–Covariance Matrix* (Ω) [a] *of the Unnormalized Regression Coefficients of Equation (5.7*) as Estimated in Table 5.2* [b]

Variable				
X2	.52			
X2X3	−.33	.29		
X10X12	.00	−.00	.00	
X14	−.03	.03	.00	.23

a. The elements of this matrix, Ω are given by the equation:
$$\Omega = \sigma_u^2 \, X'X^{-1}.$$
b. All variables are as previously defined.

the variance-covariance matrix will be roughly equal to zero. This is the assumption of uncorrelated regression disturbances, i.e., nonautoregression. In only one case is the problem apparent: the error around the estimate of X2 is somewhat, though not greatly, covariant with the error around the estimate of X2 · X3. A relatively high degree of collinearity was previously established between these two variables; that their error covariances are mildly correlated is not surprising. Typically, autoregression is a problem in time-series applications, but the difficulties it may cause may be pertinent to cross-sectional applications such as the current research. Again, estimates with this statistical problem are unbiased and consistent, but they are not efficient. In summary, each of the potential problems addressed by the variance-covariance matrix, does not seem overwhelming in the present study.

A further problem which should also be examined is the potential correlation of error terms among equations. Table 5.5 presents the correlation coefficients of the error terms among the seven equations. In only one case, between (5.1) and (5.2), is the shared, unexplained variance larger than ten percent. Thus, it is possible to reject the idea that the disturbances of each equation result from the same causes.

As in earlier chapters, pairwise correlations were utilized to yield the regression results presented here. For the generation of the residual scores, weighted mean components were used where data were missing. This procedure is most appropriate only when missing data are random. Examination of the residuals for equation (5.7) indicates that European communist polities tend to have missing data on some of the independent variables, and also that these nations—Bulgaria,

TABLE 5.5. *Correlation of Error Terms Among Equations (5.1) Through (5.7*)*

	CORRELATION COEFFICIENT					
U2[a]	$(-.61)$[b]					
U3	.04	.09				
U4	$(-.37)$	.22	.00			
U5	$-.04$	.08	.13	$-.02$		
U6	$-.22$	$-.14$	$-.12$	.29	$-.24$	
U7	.17	.03	$-.19$	.00	$-.18$	$-.22$
	U1	U2	U3	U4	U5	U6

a. Nomenclature follows the numbering of equations: U2 is the variance in the dependent variable of equation (5.2), i.e., X4 (UNVRSTY), which is unexplained by the independent variables in that equation.
b. Correlations which indicate more than ten percent of shared, *unexplained* variance are denoted by parentheses.

Czechoslavakia, East Germany, Hungary, Poland, Romania, and the Soviet Union—have patterned residual variance. Specifically, residual scores for these seven countries all have a negative sign, indicating considerably less actual inequality than predicted by the model. Furthermore, these residuals are large, each more than two standard deviations from the regression line.

The exact meaning of these findings is difficult to unravel, although their salience is easily established. There are two problems, one methodological, the other substantive. It may be, simply, that the missing data estimation procedure is inappropriate for these communist countries. More likely, and substantively important from a political perspective, is the possibility that the analyses herein presented fail to reflect accurately the confluence of variables which impinge upon inequality in nonmarket economies. It is impossible to separate the methodological from the substantive puzzlement without additional research. Until such research is undertaken, generalization about the political economy of inequality in nonmarket economic systems must be undertaken cautiously.

The relative impact of the two sets of variables, internal and external, as well as the nonsignificance of the previously important policy variables suggest another question that should be addressed. The above theory does not directly imply that either external or internal variables are more important in affecting the level of inequality within a polity. However, it is predicted that the domestic model should operate less efficiently within those polities that are higher in the hierarchy. It seems clear, however, that the omission of either set of variables may have two types of results: (1) the impact of the included variables will be somewhat exaggerated, and (2) a sizable porportion of variance will be left unexplained. Based on all of these considerations, it seems fruitful to examine the relative potency of internal versus external variables in predicting to varying levels of inequality.

In a brief and somewhat inconclusive manner this may be done by comparing the cumulative independent effects of each set on the dependent variable. For example, by examining the beta coefficients it is apparent that the significant internal variables each have an impact in the range of 0.5 standard units. The external variables which were entered into equation (5.7*) have more variant impacts: one is 0.3 and the other, 0.94. Thus, it might be argued that, *in toto,* the cumulative impacts of each set are roughly equal in magnitude, but that the external set had the individual variable of the greatest importance.

A more direct test may be accomplished by the use of hierarchical regression. Since the notion of hierarchy is essential to the research undertaken herein, and thus to avoid confusion, the term blocked, multiple stepwise regression is introduced. Briefly, what this technique allows is the specification of the order in which variables are entered into the OLS estimation procedure. Thus, it is possible to specify that the internal variables are entered as a block into the prediction equation prior to the entry of the external block of variables. By juxtaposing the order of entry, it is possible to determine more about the relative influence of each set of variables upon the dependent variable. Such an estimation procedure was undertaken and the results are presented in Table 5.6.

In the first stage, shown in Part A of Table 5.6, external variables are forced into the equation (Step 1). Each external variable has an independent contribution to the total explained variance of around thirty percent. The equation itself, with only external variables included, has an overall F-statistic of 46.8, which is highly significant. The second step (2) forces the internal variables into the equation. Essentially this may be thought of as using the residuals from Step 1 to regress upon X2 and X2·X3. The growth variable (X2) does not significantly add to the explained variance, and X2·X3 adds roughly nine percent—a signifi-

TABLE 5.6. *Blocked, Stepwise (Hierarchical) Estimation of Internal and External Determinants of Inequality in 120 Contemporary Polities*[a]

Dependent Variable : Y

STEP	INDEPENDENT VARIABLE	F TO ENTER/REMOVE	SIGNIFICANCE	$\bar{R^2}$	CHANGE R2	OVERALL F	p=
A							
1	X10X12	3.1	.081	.34	.34	46.8	.000
1	X14	45.3	.000	.65	.32		
2	X2	19.8	.000	.66	.01	37.4	.000
2	X2X3	18.5	.000	.76	.09		
B							
1	X2	19.8	.000	.03	.03	10.5	.000
1	X2X3	18.7	.000	.30	.27		
2	X14	55.6	.000	.73	.43	37.4	.000
2	X10X12	5.5	.023	.76	.03		

a. All variables as previously defined in Note a, Table 5.1, page 145. For extensive definitions, see Appendix B.

[160]

cant contribution. The overall F-statistic, when both sets or blocks of variables are included, reduces to 37.4, again, highly significant, but less than the Step 1 F-statistic.

The second stage, Part B in Table 5.5, reverses the order in which blocks of variables are entered. The overall F-statistic for this step is 10.5. Roughly thirty percent of the variance is added by these two internal variables, although of that, only three percent is unique to the growth variable (X2). Using the residuals of the internal block to regress upon the external variables, over forty-five percent of variance is additionally explained. The F-statistic corresponding to this second step is 37.4.

One appropriate test of the statistical significance of the influx of M variables to an equation with k − M variables is given by the F distribution, defined as follows:

$$F = \frac{SSadded/M}{SSresidual/(N-k-1)}$$
Where SS = sum of squares
N = the number of cases

Irrespective of the order in which variables are forced into the regression, the F-statistic is statistically significant for both steps. In Part A, external then internal variables are stepped into the predicting equation. The addition of internal variables yields an F-value of 9.7. In the juxtaposed situation, the F-value is 42.7. Each is statistically significant at the 0.000 level, thus indicating the independent saliency of each set of variables. Nonetheless, the F-values are vastly different, and it appears that the external variables not only explain more of the overall variance, regardless of order, but that their influx yields an F-value roughly five times the F-value obtained by introducing internal variables on the second step. All of this suggests the relative potency of the two sets of explanatory factors: external variables are the most potent in jointly explaining variance in internal inequality. This finding corroborates the relative nonsignificance of the internal policy variables when international variables are also considered. It also lends support to the notion that international variables may not only be important in explaining political phenomena within the polity, but also that these external factors may in certain cases be of greater importance than internal factors.

REFERENCES

Alger, C. and D. Hoovler (1974). "The Feudal Structure of Systems of International Organizations." Paper presented to the International Peace Research Association, Varanasi, India.

Alger, C. and S. Brams (1967). "Patterns of Representation in National Capitals and International Organizations." World Politics, Vol. 19, No. 4, pp 646-664.

Baumgartner, T. (1976). "Systemic Implications of Financial Flows Between Oil Exporting and Importing Countries." Paper prepared for the annual meetings of the Midwest Peace Science Association, Chicago, Illinois.

Baumgartner, T., W. Buckley, and T. Burns (1975a). "Toward a Systems Theory of Unequal Exchange, Uneven Development and Dependency Relationships." Paper prepared for the Third International Congress of Cybernetics and Systems, Budapest, Hungary.

Baumgartner, T. and T. Burns (1975b). "The Structuring of International Economic Relations." International Studies Quarterly. Vol. 19, No. 2, pp 126-159.

Brams, S. (1966). "Transaction Flows in the International System." American Political Science Review, Vol. 60, No. 4, pp 888-898.

Buckley, W. (1967). Sociology and Modern Systems Theory, Englewood Cliffs, New Jersey: Prentice-Hall.

Dos Santos, T. (1970). "The Structure of Dependence." American Economic Review, Vol. 60, No. 2, pp 231-236.

Duvall, R. (1975). International Stratification: Concept and Theory. Unpublished Ph.D. dissertation. Northwestern University.

Duvall, R. and B. Russett (1976). "Some Proposals to Guide Empirical Research on Contemporary Imperialism." Jerusalem Journal of International Relations, Vol. 6, No. 2, pp 1-27.

Eckstein, H. and T. Gurr (1975). Patterns of Authority. New York: John Wiley.

Furtado, C. (1970). Economic Development of Latin America: A Survey from Colonial Times to the Cuban Revolution. Cambridge: Cambridge University Press.

Galtung, J. (1971). "A Structural Theory of Imperialism." Journal of Peace Research, Vol. 7, No. 2, pp 81-117.

Gurr, T. and R. Duvall (1973). "Civic Conflict in the 1960s: A Reciprocal Theoretical System with Parameter Estimates." Comparative Political Studies, Vol. 6, No. 2, pp 135-169.

Harary, F. (1953-1954). "On the Notion of Balance of a Signed Graph." Michigan Mathematical Journal, Vol. 2, pp 143-146.

Harary, F. and H. Miller (1970). "A Graph Theoretic Approach to the Analysis of International Relations." Journal of Conflict Resolution, Vol. 14, No. 1, pp 57-63.

Hart, J. (1974). "Structures of Influence and Cooperation-Conflict." International Interaction, Vol. 1, pp 141-162.

Kaplan, M. (1957). System and Process in International Politics. New York: John Wiley.

Kmenta, J. (1970). Elements of Econometrics. New York: Macmillan.

Modelski, G. (1973). "Conflict Stability and Intergovernment Elite Networks: A Study of World Order in 1965." Paper presented to the IXth World Congress, International Political Science Association, Montreal, Canada.

Morgenthau, H. (1956). Politics among Nations. New York: Knopf.

[162]

Piaget, J. (1970). Structuralism. New York: Basic Books, translated by C. Maschler.

Rockwell, R. (1973). "Assessment of Multicollinearity: the Haitovsky Test of the Determinant." Sociological Methods and Research, Vol. 3, pp 308-320.

Russett, B. (1967). International Regions and the International System: A Study in Political Ecology. Chicago, Illinois: Rand McNally and Co.

Simon, H. (1969). The Sciences of the Artificial. Cambridge, Massachusetts: M.I.T. Press.

Skjelsbaek, N. (1969). "Development of the Systems of International Organization: A Diachronic Study." Paper presented to the International Peace Research Association meeting.

Sunkel, O. (1969). "National Development Policy and External Dependence in Latin America." Journal of Development Studies, No. 4, pp 23-48.

Tucker, R. (1975). "Oil: The Issue of American Intervention." Commentary, Vol. 59, pp 21-31.

Summary and Conclusions

6

6.1 RECAPITULATION

This cross-sectional study of some 120 contemporary polities focuses on the political-economic determinants of inequality. The domestic characteristics of national political systems and their policies are explored for their influence on the level of inequality within each nation state. Additionally, the characteristics of the international system as a whole and that of its most dominant members, the superpowers, are examined as potential determinants of inequality. The framework in which these two facets are analyzed, a theory of hierarchical interaction, is developed from a synthesis of prior work in the economic, sociological, and political sciences.

Previous work on the topic of inequality has tended to be restrictive in that not only has it attempted to explain inequality solely in terms of economic determinants, but it also has rarely searched beyond the boundaries of the nation state for its major causes. Typical explorations ignored the conglomerate effects of many potential causes which are not only resident within the polity, but also characteristic of the international system. Herein, an attempt is made to address these issues as directly as possible. In seeking a plausible explanation of variant levels of inequality, this research has endeavored to build upon the work of others by integrating some specific propositions which have shown prior theoretical and empirical promise. Expanding beyond this, the theoretical framework developed speaks not only to the international social structure, but in addition to the inequality structured from within the polity.

The measurement strategy used to assess the level of inequality within contemporary polities itself has important implications. As noted earlier, the issues involved in measuring inequality have proved intriguing from a wide latitude of perspectives. The most commonly accepted measure is the Gini index. This measure has been accused of many shortcomings, including insensitivity to: (1) work-age cycles, (2) unemployment, (3) family *versus* individual income, (4) investment earnings, (5) land holdings, (6) barter arrangements, (7) inheritances, and (8) biased tax reportage, as well as many others.[1] As is well known, historical and cross-sectional data of the type necessary to construct even crude Gini indices are largely unavailable; the search for a large body of the type of data required to introduce all of these "controls" is quixotic.

Empirical examination of sectorally calculated Gini indices (GINISECT) and scores obtained from individual level income data (GININDIV) showed as close a pattern to randomness as one is likely to find. The covariation of the individual level index with other independent measures which also purport to measure inequality was uniformly high. Sectoral Gini scores were found to be unrelated to virtually every other currently available measure of the aggregate level of inequality within polities. This finding alone casts much doubt upon prior work which employed sector-based Gini scores as an approximation of income inequality. It also introduces a certain amount of incommensurability between earlier work and the current study.

The exact measure used in this study was a composite of several highly correlated measures of inequality which were constructed independently of one another. Among these was one which has large potential for use in replication of this and other studies, as well as in more longitudinally designed research. The ratio of poverty to affluence was taken as an indicator of the aggregate level of inequality within polities.[2] The argument upon which this index is based is simple; a high degree of affluence and a high degree of poverty is characteristic of, and thereby indicates, the existence of relatively unequal distribution of social product; to the extent that poverty and affluence are more equally balanced, there is less inequality; and, to the extent that neither a great deal of poverty nor affluence is present, there is even less inequality.

In the cross-section studied here, the ratio indicator is highly covariant with the other independent indices of inequality. Moreover, each of the subconcepts, poverty and affluence, represents variables for which historical data are theoretically available. Thus, longitudinal studies might use the proposed ratio to track the levels of inequality within various polities. Needless to say, the exact measures of affluence and poverty will themselves change over time: the number of motor vehicle deaths in eighteenth-century France indicates absolutely nothing about the extent of affluence within that polity. The average price of bread, on the other hand, might indicate a great deal about the level of poverty. A case in point is the work of Snyder and Tilly (1976), which has used food prices to measure and study economic deprivation as a stimulus to collective violence in France from 1830 to 1960. It is not necessary to catalogue a variety of potential indicators of poverty and affluence in a variety of contexts to illustrate the potential manifest in this strategy.

One important corollary to the use of this ratio index is that it does not necessarily focus upon the monetary aspects of social product: more than income distribution may be tapped. Thus, this index fits within the framework of an indicator approach to monitoring, and alleviating, social problems and development. From the American nationalist perspective, the social indicators movement is well known. There are also at least two proposed systems which seek to provide surveillance of social conditions across the globe. One is a project spearheaded by Galtung (1975), which carries with it an approach which has been picked up in the basic needs orientation of the ILO. The other is the global monitoring system suggested in the writings of Snyder, Hermann, and Lasswell (1976). Indicators of inequality are important to these types of projects, whatever their political orientation, and the measures suggested here might prove useful not only in monitoring future trends, but in anchoring that understanding of the future in studies of the past. It should also be pointed out that this ratio of wealth to poverty presents the two main components of inequality itself. Furthermore, each component may be separately addressed by policy makers in attempts to change the level of inequality.

The notion that development is associated with inequality has received considerable and frequent attention in the scholarly literature. Planners and scholars alike have often disagreed on the direction of this association: some propose a positive linkage, while others argue

[166]

equally forcefully for the opposite. Based upon the theoretical and empirical work in this study, it may be said that each position has considerable merit. Turning to the domestic aspects, the level of *per capita* development, measured either by gross national product or energy consumption, tends to be characteristic of polities with lower levels of aggregate inequality. This association is a strong one; moreover, there is apparently a threshold beyond which, however, decrements to inequality are not correspondent with increments in development. The most dramatic aspect of this relationship is that it appears to be much stronger within groups of polities which have relatively low levels of *per capita* development than it is for polities with low levels of inequality. This elicits the idea that the relationship is potentially curvilinear in form. Nonetheless, the first-order effects of high levels of development are lower levels of inequality.

That the level of development is strongly associated with less inequality seems clear, yet indices of relatively medium-term growth in economic strength are themselves highly related to more rather than less inequality. Thus, it appears that growth is not directly translated into more equality. This seems plausible on the argument that one should expect a short-term accumulation of new product into new sectors, largely urban and industrial. Such a short-run influence would directly lead to more inequality. Neither of these two arguments relating aspects of development to inequality necessarily draw one either to the position that development itself leads to reductions, or to the stance that it directly provokes more inequality. These separate conclusions have been drawn, too often, in the past.

Taken jointly, the arguments suggest that the level of development tends to alleviate inequality, while growth in the level of development tends to aggravate it. The linkages between the growth and level of development are not explored in depth in a cross-sectional study such as this. It does appear, however, that one mechanism clearly is involved in the relationship between these aspects of development and its connection with inequality: the diversity of the infrastructure of the economy. An economy able to generate new product within a wide range of sectors will also tend to spread that increased product throughout the economy in a fairly direct and rapid fashion, thus achieving, other things being equal, diminished levels of inequality.

Irrespective of their interrelationships, these three aspects of development have independent effects on the distribution of valued goods within the polity. Growth may be associated with heightened inequality, while growth which obtains within a structurally diversified framework is associated with less inequality, as is the level of development.

Economists who posed arguments relating various aspects of economic development to inequality have tended to rely heavily upon political and sociological factors in their explanations. Subsequently, both political scientists and sociologists have come to utilize these arguments without much amplification on the latent political and sociological components of the economic analyses. Two areas have borne the brunt of such imprecision: (1) mass participation and political mobilization, and (2) the extent of policy effort aimed at redistribution. Based more upon qualitative than quantitative evidence, it has been argued in the past that the link between development and inequality is mediated by policy efforts.

Economic product does not magically transform itself into increased productivity for all members of society. Policies must be undertaken which attempt to promote that transformation. The Scandanavian countries, for example, have long been recognized as being among the most egalitarian in the world. They also have a wide range of experience with social welfare policy, ranging from extensive social security programs first established in the 1900s to graduated income tax schemes directed at redistributing personal earnings back toward the mean. Education policy has also been promoted as one of the primary ways in which the modern state may seek to equalize the distribution of knowledge and skills, and thereby insure access to a wider range of more productive and efficient jobs. Thus, investment in school programs by governments presumably has large returns in terms of decreasing inequality. When only domestic factors are considered, the impact of each of these types of policy effort, both schooling and social welfare, on the level of inequality is considerable. While one might suspect that political mobilization is itself related to the existence of such policy effort, this turns out not to be the case: political mobilization is unrelated to either the existence or intensity of such programs.

On the national politics side, three potential causes of inequality are explored: (1) the level of development (2) the short-term growth of the economy, and (3) the diversity of the infrastructure. Policy efforts in social welfare programs are introduced as a mediating variable upon the hypothesized relationships; political mobilization is examined for

[168]

its potential catalytic effect upon public policy. On the whole, considerable empirical support is found for a model of the domestic determinants of inequality.

The influx of explanatory propositions which are international in scope considerably complicates the clarity introduced by the nature of solely domestic frameworks. The contemporary international system is characterized by a feudal hierarchy in which is embedded the mechanisms necessary to reproduce and maintain that hierarchy. Nations ranking high within that hierarchy tend to have a greater amount of domestic as well as international resources available to them. The possession of these resources allows them, in part, to structure their interactions with polities lower in the hierarchy. The type, frequency, and the implications of the interactions are each structured to benefit those within higher tiers in the international system. This structuring of interaction in turn causes resources to flow out of the lower elements into the higher ones. Nations able to structure their interactions have correspondingly wider latitude in their interactions with those at low levels in the hierarchy. In short, not only is the hierarchy predicated upon international inequalities, but it is inherently self-reinforcing of the extant hierarchical boundaries.

In summary, the interrelationship between a polity's level of inequality and various aspects of its international interactions was strong. The position held by a nation within the international hierarchy is conditioned by, and itself conditions, the extent to which the polity possesses resources within both the domestic and international environment. The possession of these resources promotes the structuring of interactions so that they are differentially advantageous to members within the various tiers of the hierarchy. Importantly, this constrains the domestic translation of product into distribution patterns. Moreover, global characteristics have direct linkages to the level of inequality in that the possession of meta-resources and the extent of interaction latitude both lead to different levels of inequality within different tiers of the hierarchy. When the international explanations are introduced into the model, the domestic policy linkages diminish in importance—indicating the statistical potency of international *vis-a-vis* domestic explanations of the levels of inequality within contemporary polities.

The consequences of this system for the domestic distribution of valued goods is considerable. In short, there are structures which lie behind the distribution of goods. These structures reproduce and maintain themselves, both domestically and internationally. Most direct is the impact which the international hierarchy makes on the extent of resources which are available for distribution within the polity. The structure tends to remove product and resources from polities low in the hierarchy and to transmit them to those high in the structure. Thus, the hierarchy places tight constraints upon the economic and political mechanisms which are said to translate product into more (or less) inequality. Quite simply, these domestic mechanisms, including policy, do not seem to be as efficient in low hierarchy polities.

6.2 DISCUSSION AND IMPLICATIONS

Having summarized the main results of this study in the previous section, it remains to discuss these findings in terms of their political and research implications. This is especially important in terms of the many puzzling factors which are suggested by the various results.

The arguments about the determinants of inequality made in this book are primarily based upon two sources of information: (1) cross-sectional, empirical evidence present in this study, and (2) the cumulative work of many other scholars who have also been constrained to work within a cross-sectional, as opposed to longitudinal, mode of analysis. The fundamental reason underlying this one-sided research is, of course, the unavailability of adequate time series data on the levels of inequality in polities.

This concentration on cross-sections raises several questions. How has the nonlongitudinal imperative diverted attention from an understanding of the underlying processes which govern these phenomena? More important still is the political question of how policy efforts aimed at redistribution may have been ''misdirected'' by the potentially erroneous cross-sectional generalities. Kuh (1959) and, more recently, Brunner and Liepelt (1972) have each written pioneering articles pointing out some of the problems with cross-sectional-to-longitudinal inference. How can the results offered here be made commensurate with the known difficulties?

First, it should be pointed out that the evidence presented here is nonexperimental. This means that the theory and its implications are bounded by the available data. Thus, new developments in any or all of

[170]

the economic and political mechanisms that are argued to be determinants of inequality will potentially have effects which are not predicted by the model. An innovative policy mechanism, for example, may have a large impact on inequality. Moreover, drastic system changes, such as the shocks brought about by OPEC's price quadrupling of 1973 may cause the system to distribute goods in a radically different fashion. The impact of such changes cannot be foretold solely from the theory and the data utilized here. More specifically, dynamic changes in the international hierarchy fall as yet outside of this theoretical framework.

There is considerable evidence that cross-sectional and longitudinal analyses of the inequality question do tend to yield similar results. Evidence for this is presented by several aspects of the results in this, and other, studies. First, development components pertinent to the model have been explored in both cross-sectional and longitudinal contexts and were found to be similarly reflected in each. That is the cross-sectional evidence about development *per se,* is homomorphic to the evidence gleaned from longitudinal analysis.

Beyond that aspect of the model, the striking similarity of Jackman's results (1974:37) on development and inequality with those presented in Chapter Three, Tables 3.1 and 3.2 (p. 000) must be considered as replicative. Thus two independent, cross-sectional estimations of the same model, as measured independently in polities some ten years apart (1960 and 1970), produced remarkably congruent results. This also provides additional evidence for the longitudinal "stability" of the cross-sectional results. However, the full model has not been so replicated.

Another important aspect of the cross-sectional longitudinal question that must be considered is the relative dynamics of the variables in the model. Almost all evidence yet presented has suggested that there has been very little change in inequality levels in the past twenty years. Thus, it seems likely that inequality patterns present a fairly stable structure of relationships that may be captured by cross-sectional modeling. It is hoped that longitudinal analyses may be mounted in the near future. The strategy of indexing the level of inequality by measuring the ratio of rich to poor, of affluence to poverty, may be very useful toward this goal.

Even granting for the moment the cross-sectional to longitudinal inference, there has been little visible change in inequality as reflected

[171]

FIGURE 6.1. The Relationship Between Gross National Product *Per Capita* and the Percentage Income Share Held by the Top 20 and Bottom 40 Percent of the Population*

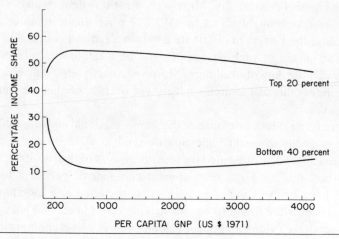

* Empirically estimated equations taken from Chenery *et al.* (1974) p. 15.

in what little time series data are available. Politically, the inference to be drawn from the cross-sectional evidence would extend this prognosis well into the future. In terms of the wealth held by the top and bottom segments of the cumulative population, Figure 6.1 presents a graphic illustration of this conclusion. Beyond very minimal development levels, say $200 GNP *per capita,* neither the absolute nor the relative shares of the wealth, held by the very rich or the very poor in a particular polity are inferred to change drastically. This implies not only that policy efforts may well be ineffectual in many individual countries, but also that the division of the globe into different worlds, in terms of both development and equality, is unlikely to be much different in twenty to thirty years than it is today. The polities which, according to the theory and evidence presented here, stand the best chance of altering inequality levels are the poorest ones.

Thus, the rich *versus* poor dichotomy at both the domestic and international level is very likely to be maintained for the future. Change may only be possible through major systemic transformations of the type often suggested under the rubric of a New International Economic Order. Moreover, change may only be likely in a few selected nations.

Related to the cross-sectional versus longitudinal question are the multitude of issues raised by the arguments of many dependency theorists. These ideas were introduced in Chapter Four and will not be repeated here. Suffice it to say that the dependency idea is, with some simplification, a matter of structure generating behavior, as opposed to the behavioral orientation of structure being generated by patterns of behavior. The dependency arguments may be correct in suggesting not one model but two. The first would be applicable to dependent nations; the second, to polities which are interdependent. Roughly, these two categories correspond to the different tiers in the international feudal hierarchy. Whether nations can move from the status of an LDC and its attendant processes and governing structure to the position of a DC is a problematic assertion. Liberal theorists tend to argue the affirmative, while dependency theorists and most Marxists would argue the contrary.

This characterization implies that even given that the possibility for changes in inequality of LDC nations is greater than the corresponding possibility of such change in DCs, the "distortion," i.e., dependence, introduced by the international division of labor in the world economic structure may make such change virtually impossible. Accordingly, it may be possible that the domestic components of the political economy of inequality may be appropriate for polities high in the international hierarchy, while the international aspects of these processes are primarily pertinent only for the polities low in that feudally organized system.

In addition to the questions of (1) cross-section *versus* longitudinal evidence and (2) dependency theory, the policy issue is of crucial relevance as well. Policy effort has been defined in terms of social insurance programs, notably unemployment policies, and educational programs. Such a delimitation of policy may be unduly biased toward Western, industrial polities. That is, social welfare, in most countries, has been defined not in terms of basic survival needs of the populace but in terms of institutional response to economic and political problem areas such as unemployment. Thus, policy, as herein defined, may leave the bulk of the population in certain countries, e.g., rural agricultural, untouched no matter how institutionally "successful" it is. Again, these rural agricultural polities are low in the international hierarchy and as such represent the group of nations which may have the best chance of introducing policies which could be fruitful in reducing the level of societal inequality.

[173]

One last consideration which should also be addressed in future work deals with the strong inadequacy of the theory (and the data) to make relatively accurate predictions in the case of communist polities. Throughout, the level of inequality in these polities has been significantly underestimated by the various forms of the theory, ranging from the domestic to the international side. This strongly suggests that crucial elements are misspecified or omitted from the model. One fruitful area worthy of attention here would be the role of socialist revolutions in explaining differences in societal inequality. Case studies of countries like China, Cuba, and Tanzania might well prove valuable in untangling the differences that exist between bourgeois and capitalist societies with respect to the level of societal inequality.

N O T E S

1. One pertinent criticism of studying inequality in general is that offered by J. Pen (1971). It remains one of the most readable and critical essays on this topic.
2. Peter Wiles has forcefully argued for a similar strategy:

    It is not, then, simply that the Gini coefficient is insensitive to extremes, uncertain in its reaction at all times, and a mere average where averaging is least appropriate. . . . By concentrating on the decile and if possible semidecile ratio I see now that I am drawing attention to a radical cleavage in the tasks of those who study distribution. . . . If data were available I would always take the average of the top decile (which gives explicit weight to millionaires) ÷ the average of the bottom decile (which includes all the old, unemployed, and sick . . .). It follows that one of the most despised (and simple!) of all measures of inequality, the "range" or (the highest income − the lowest) ÷ the mean . . . is one of the best. Alone among the indices commonly discussed, it points us in the right direction [1975:ix,xff].

R E F E R E N C E S

Brunner, R.D. and K. Liepelt (1972). "Data Analysis, Process Analysis, and System Change." Midwest Journal of Political Science, Vol. 16, pp 538-569.

Galtung, J., A. Guha, A. Wirak, S. Sjilie, M. Cifuentes, and H. Goldstein (1975). "Measuring World Development." parts I and II, Alternatives: A Journal of World Policy, Vol. 1, Nos. 1 and 4, pp, 131-158, 523-555.

Kuh, E. (1959). "The Validity of Cross-Sectionally Estimated Behavior Equations in Time Series Applications." Econometrica, Vol. 27, pp 197-214.

Pen, J. (1971). Income Distribution: Facts, Theories, Policies, New York: Praeger Publishers.

Snyder, D. and C. Tilly (1972). "Hardship and Collective Violence in France, 1830 to 1960." American Sociological Review, Vol. 37, pp 520-532.

Snyder, R., C. Hermann, and H. Lasswell (1976). "A Global Monitoring System: Appraising the Effects of Government on Human Dignity." International Studies Quarterly, Vol. 20, No. 2, pp 221-260.

Wiles, P. (1974). Distribution of Income: East and West, New York: American Elsevier.

APPENDIX A
Country Names, Acronyms, and Identification Numbers

Acronym	Number	Country Name
AFG	1	Afghanistan
ALB	2	Albania
ALG	3	Algeria
ANG	4	Argentina
AUL	5	Australia
AUS	6	Austria
BEL	7	Belgium
BOL	8	Bolivia
BOT	9	Botswana
BRA	10	Brazil
BHO	11	Belize
BUL	12	Bulgaria
BUR	13	Burma
BRD	14	Burundi
CAM	15	Cambodia
CAO	16	Cameroon
CAN	17	Canada
CAR	18	Central African Republic
CEY	19	Sri Lanka
CHA	20	Chad
CHI	21	Chile
CHN	22	Peoples Republic of China

Acronym	Number	Country Name
CHT	23	Taiwan
COL	24	Colombia
CON	25	Congo (Brazzaville)
COS	26	Costa Rica
CUB	27	Cuba
CYP	28	Cyprus
CZE	29	Czechoslavakia
DAH	30	Benin
DEN	31	Denmark
DOM	32	Dominican Republic
ECU	33	Ecuador
EGY	34	Egypt
ELS	35	El Salvador
ETH	36	Ethiopia
FIN	37	Finland
FRN	38	France
GAB	39	Gabon
GAM	40	Gambia
GMW	41	Germany, West
GME	42	Germany, East
GHA	43	Ghana
GRC	44	Greece
GUA	45	Guatamala
GUI	46	Guinea
HON	47	Honduras
HOK	48	Hong Kong
HUN	49	Hungary
ICE	50	Iceland
IND	51	India
INS	52	Indonesia
IRN	53	Iran
IRQ	54	Iraq
IRE	55	Ireland
ISR	56	Israel
ITA	57	Italy
IVO	58	Ivory Coast
JAM	59	Jamaica
JAP	60	Japan
JOR	61	Jordan

Acronym	Number	Country Name
KEN	62	Kenya
KON	63	North Korea
KOS	64	South Korea
LAO	65	Laos
LEB	66	Lebanon
LES	67	Lesotho
LIB	68	Liberia
LBY	69	Libya
LUX	70	Luxembourg
MGY	71	Malagasy
MLW	72	Malawi
MLY	73	Malasia
MEX	74	Mexico
MRC	75	Morocco
NET	76	Netherlands
NEW	77	New Zealand
NIC	78	Nicaragua
NIG	79	Niger
NGA	80	Nigeria
NOR	81	Norway
PAK	82	Pakistan
PAN	83	Panama
PAR	84	Paraguay
PER	85	Peru
PHI	86	Philippines
POL	87	Poland
POR	88	Portugal
PUE	89	Puerto Rico
ROM	90	Romania
SAU	91	Saudi Arabia
SEN	92	Senegal
SIE	93	Sierra Leone
SIN	94	Singapore
SOM	95	Somalia
SAF	96	South Africa
SPA	97	Spain
SUD	98	Sudan
SWE	99	Sweden
SWI	100	Switzerland

Acronym	Number	Country Name
SYR	101	Syria
TAN	102	Tanzania
TAI	103	Thailand
TUN	104	Tunisia
TUR	105	Turkey
UNK	106	United Kingdom
USR	107	United Soviet Socialist Republics
USA	108	United States
UGA	109	Uganda
VOL	110	Upper Volta
URU	111	Uruguay
VEN	112	Venezeula
VTN	113	North Vietnam
VTS	114	South Vietnam
YEN	115	North Yemen
YES	116	South Yemen
YUG	117	Yugoslavia
ZAI	118	Zaire
ZAM	119	Zambia
ZIM	120	Zimbabwe

APPENDIX B
List of Variables, Definitions, and Sources in the Order of Their Appearance in the Text

This appendix documents each of the variables utilized in this study. For each variable, several pieces of information are included:

1. the acronyms and identifiers associated with each variable for which data was collected
2. a brief, substantive description of the variable
3. the year(s) to which the data pertain
4. the source(s) used in collecting the data
5. computational formula, if any
6. the section in the text in which the variable is first discussed.

Introduced in Section:　　　　　　　　　　**List of Variables**

2.41　　　　　　**GINISECT**—a sector-based Gini index of income inequality; classically calculated using circa 1970 data on two subvariables, size of the work force in each sector and gross domestic product generated in each sector; data on the later were mostly taken from *Yearbook of National Accounts Statistics* (1973), volume III; data on the former come from a multitude of sources: *Yearbook of Labour Statistics*, 1972 and 1973, various Army Area Handbooks, the *Economic Survey of Asia and the Far East*, 1973, and the *Survey of Economic Conditions in Africa*, 1972.

2.41　　　　　　**GININDIV**—a classically computed Gini index based upon the income shares held by the top twenty, middle forty, and lower forty percents of the population; data are mostly ca. 1970, and were initially collated from various country studies by S. Jain in, *Size Distribution of Income; A World Bank Publication*, 1975.

[180]

2.42   SOCIMOB—a measure of the extent of social immobility within a polity; explicitly defined in Table 2.4; obtained from T. Gurr and R. Duvall, *Nations in Conflict*, forthcoming.

2.43   HIBBZSCR—a measure of inequality which uses infant mortality (INFMORT) from the *United Nations Demographic Yearbook*, 1973, the number of doctors per 10,000 inhabitants from the *World Health Statistics Annual*, 1970, the number of kilocalories per head per day (KILOCAL) and the percentage of daily requirements per head (REQPCT) which each are 1969–71 averages taken from the United Nations Food Conference: *Assessment of World Food Situation*, 1974; REQPCT includes a ten percent waste factor and a correction for additional "psychological" requirements; these four variables were standardized and added together to form HIBBZSCR.

2.44   INEQ2—inequality index by a ratio of poverty (POVRTY) to affluence (AFFLU); explicitly defined in Table 2.3; POVERTY itself was indexed by standardizing three variables, KILOCAL, REQPCT, and the grams of protein per head per day (PROTEIN), averaged for 1969–71, taken from the same source as HIBBZSCR; AFFLU was similarly constructed using the number of luxury Hilton Hotels within the polity (HILTON), taken from Trans World Airlines, TWA *Ambassador*, 1974, the number of universities and colleges (UNVRSTY) reported in *International Handbook of Universities and Other Institutions of Higher Instruction*, 1974, and the number of motor-vehicle deaths per 100,000 inhabitants given in "Motor Vehicle Deaths, 1969," *World Health Statistics Report*, 26, No 10, 1973.

2.44   INEQ1—a measure of inequality of telephone service; catalogued by dividing the average number of telephones per 100 inhabitants in 1970 by the average number of phones per 100 inhabitants in the capital city; data reported in *The World's Telephones*, 1971.

2.5   INEQUAL (Y)—a summary index of inequality using HIBBZSCR, INEQ1, INEQ2, SOCIMOB, and GININDIV; composite Z-score was calculated using equation (2.9).

3.2   ENGCON (X1)—a measure of the level of development; data is the 1970 per capita consumption of million metric tons of coal equivalents; obtained from the *United Nations' Statistical Yearbook*, 1972.

3.3   IXCONS (X2)—a longitudinal summary of the growth in construction activity (1963 = 100) over an eleven-year period which is normalized so that maximum IXCONS = 1.0; *Yearbook of Construction Statistics* 1963–72.

[181]

3.3   **DIVERSTY (X3)**—an index of the diversity of the economic infrastructure; calculated by summing squared proportions of sector work force and gross domestic product, subtracting each sum from 1.0, and then dividing the work force concentration by the concentration of GDP; same basic data as used in construction of GINISECT.

4.3   **UNVRSTY (X4)**—a measure of educational policy; the number of colleges or universities in each polity. *International Handbook of Universities and Other Institutes of Higher Education*, 6th Ed.

4.3   **UNEMFAC (X5)**—an index of the social security policy in the unemployment area; a factor analysis (Table 4.2) was performed on aspects of social security programs in three areas, unemployment, work injury, and old age compensation (defined explicity in Table 4.1) and the factor score for the unemployment factor was used; all data used in the factor analysis and the resultant index comes from *Social Security Programs Throughout the World*, 1973, Research Report no. 44, The Social Security Administration, Washington, DC.

4.4   **POLMOB (X6)**—an index of political mobilization which is the addition of the Z-scores of two components, the size of the communist party as a portion of the total population, obtained from *World Data Handbook*, General Foreign Policy Series No. 264, U.S. State Department, 1972, and an index of the extent of democracy (DEMOC), defined in Table 4.3.

5.4   **HRRCHY (X10)**—a measure of the level occupied by a polity in the international feudal hierarchy based upon diplomatic representation; obtained from F. Abolfathi (1978) *Determinants of Military Spending: Description, Analysis, and Forecasts*, Ph.D. dissertation, Northwestern University

5.4   **SUPTRD (X11)**—a measure of trade interaction with both the United States and the Soviet Union; percent of total exports which go to either superpower is added to the percent of imports coming from either; data is for 1970, and was taken from a variety of sources: *International Monetary Fund Direction of Trade: 1966–70*, R. Kanet's article in E. Mickievitz *Handbook of Soviet Social Science Data*, New York: The Free Press, 1970.

5.4   **ALLMNCS (X12)**—measure of international resources resident within the polity; the number of multinational companies ca. 1968 is taken from the *Yearbook of International Organizations*.

5.4   **GALTUNG (X13)**—trade-composition index for 1970 commodity export data; from *The United Nations Yearbook of International Trade Statistics*, volume 1, 1974.

[182]

5.4   **XDVRSTY (X14)**—index of trade latitude which assesses a nation's absolute deviation from aggregate world trade picture, by commodity; 1968 data taken from *Handbook of International Trade and Development Statistics, 1972.*

ADDENDA TO REFERENCES

Chapter 1.

Paukert, F. (1973). "Income Distribution at Different Levels of Development: A Survey of Evidence." International Labour Review, Vol. 108, No. 2-3, pp 97-125.

Stallings, B. (1972). Economic Dependency in Africa and Latin America. Sage Professional Paper, Comparative Politics Series, 01-031, Vol. 3, Beverly Hills, Ca.: Sage Publications.

Cline, W.R. (1975). "Distribution and Development: A Survey of the Literature." Journal of Development Economics, Vol. 1, pp 359-400.

Coser, L. (1956). The Functions of Social Conflict, London: Routledge and Kegan-Paul.

Dahrendorf, R. (1959). Class and Class Conflict in Industrial Society, Stanford, Ca.: Stanford University Press.

Chapter 2.

Herrera, A.O., H.D. Scolnik, et al. (1976). Catastrophe or New Society? A Latin American World Model, Ottawa, Canada: International Development Research Centre.

Ray, J.L. and J.D. Singer (1973). "Measuring the Concentration of Power in the International System." Sociological Methods and Research, Vol. 1, No. 4, pp 403-437.

Chapter 3.

Lenski, G. (1966). Power and Privilege: A Theory of Social Stratification, New York: McGraw-Hill.

Chapters 5 and 6.

Jackman, R. (1975). Politics and Social Equality, New York: John Wiley.

Index

Several entries refer to Notes cited within the text. The page number of the text cite is followed by two numbers within parentheses: the first indicates the specific page number within the Notes section; the second, the specific number of the Note.

A

Abolfathi, F. 35(47:16), 182
Adelman, I. 3, 11, 25, 53, 57,
    58, 86
Affluence
    Measurement of 31
Akins, J E. 9
Alger, C. 127
Alker, H. 9, 10, 23, 23(46:8)
Allison, G. 2
Althauser, R. 35(47:17)
Amin, S. 80(82:4)
Anscombe, F. 63
Axiomatic Model
    Domestic 105–107
    International 130–132

B

Baran, P. 58
Barber, B. 16
Barry, B. 3
Baumgartner, T. 121, 125, 129
Bentham, J. 12
Bonilla, F. 80(82:4)
Boudon, R. 9,13, 98
Brams, S. 121, 123, 127
Brunner, R. D. 170
Buchanan, J. 92
Buckley, W. 121, 125
Burns, T. 121, 125, 129

C

Cambell, D. T. 35–36
Caporaso, J. 80(82:4)
Cardoso, F. H. 80
Chase-Dunn, C. 3
Chenery, H. 3, 9(45:1), 10, 13, 25,
    26, 31, 59, 60, 91, 99
Chilcote, R. H. 80(82:4)
Chintakananda, I. 21, 22, 22(48:6)

Chiswick, R. R. 13, 17, 98, 99
Cline, W. R. 4
Cook, K. S. 16
Coser, L. 4
Cutright, P. 3, 23, 24, 57, 93–95, 97

D

Dahrendorf, R. 4
Daniels, N. 3
Data set
  description of 5–6
  see also Appendices A and B
de Tocqueville, A. 3, 18
Dependencia 80, 120
Deutsch, K. W. 100
Diversity
  defined 76
Dos Santos, T. 2, 80, 120
Drewnoski, J. 25
Duvall, R. 2, 3, 9, 16, 16(45:2), 20,
  23, 24,120, 121, 181

E

Echols, J. 94
Eckstein, H. 121
Elliot, C. 17
Emmanuel, A. 17

F

Faletto, E. 80
Fiske, D. W. 35–36
Frank, A. G. 80(82:4)
Furtado, C. 80(82:4), 120

G

Galtung, J. 3, 11, 12, 13, 14,
  80(82:4), 121, 125, 126,
  128, 129, 139, 148, 166
Gillespie, J. 2
Gini Index
  Operationalization of 30
Gini, C. 18–20
Girling, R. 80(82:4)
Grant, J. 14
Gurr, T. R. 3, 9, 10, 11, 18, 24,

24(46:9), 25, 31, 102, 121,
181

H

Haq, M. 14
Harary, F. 122, 128
Hart, J. 123, 128
Heberlein, T. 35(47:17)
Herfindal, O. L. 75
Hermann, C. 166
Herrera, A. O. 3, 9, 14
Hibbs, D. A. 11, 24, 31
Hibbs' Z-Score
  operationalization of 31
Hierarchy 120–124
  and detente 128
  empirical studies of 127–128
  feudal 126
  related to inequality 136, 169
Hilton, G. 63(82:2)
Hobbes, T. 12
Hoivik, T. 24
Hoovler, D. 127
Hudson, M. C. 5, 21, 25, 25(46:10),
  38

I

Inequality
  and conflict 4
  and development 4, 167–168
    and diversity of infrastructure
    72
    level of 53
    linear vs. curvilinear 65
    rapid growth in 72
  and education 9
  and international hierarchy 136,
    169
  and market organization 45
  and political threshold 56, 81
  and public policy 87
  and region 45
  consequences of 116
  definitions of 12–19
  index used in study defined 42
  measures of 19, 23–26, 34, 42
  measuring 10
  persistence of 3

International Labour Organisation
14, 25, 31

J

Jackman, R. 3, 4, 23, 23(46:7), 24,
   31, 40, 41, 53, 58, 59, 68–73,
   79–81, 94–95, 153, 171
Jaguaribe, H. 51(82:1), 80
Jain, S. 59, 180
Janda, K. 24(46:9)
Jencks, C. 98

K

Kanet, R. 182
Kaplan, M. 121
Keohane, R. 2
Kmenta, J. 63(82:2), 66(82:3), 78,
   144
Kravis, I. 74
Kuh, E. 170
Kuznets, S. 3, 6,20–22, 26, 38, 41,
   53–59, 73–74, 81(82:5),
   86–87, 101

L

Lasswell, H. 166
Lenin, V. I. 101, 120
Lenski, G. 4, 57, 73, 94
Lerner, D. 100
Levine, M. S. 24(46:9)
Liepelt, K. 170
Lipset, S. 3

M

Marshall, A. 88–90
Marx, K. 101, 120
Michels, R. 101
Mickievitz, E. 182
Miller, H. 122, 128
Mitchell, E. J. 4, 17(45:3)
Mobilization
   political 100
Modelski, G. 127–128
Morgan J. 57
Morgan, W. 16

Morgenthau, H. 134
Morris, C. 3, 11, 25, 53, 57–58, 86
Moul, W. B. 5, 51(82:1)
Myrdal, G. 54, 58, 74

N

Nagel, J. 4, 17(45:3)
Nelson, R. T. 30(46:12)
Nordhaus, W. 13
Nugent, J. 89
Nye, J. 2

O

Olson, M. 73, 92
Overseas Development Council 14

P

Paige, J. M. 17(45:3)
Paranzino, D. 17(45:3)
Participation
   political 104
      Polmob Index 102–103
Paukert, F. 3
Pen, J. 165(174:1)
Pennock, J. R. 16
Piaget, J. 5, 120
Plato 12
Policy
   social welfare 92
      SIPE Index 94–95
      Social Security programs 93, 97
Poverty-affluence ratio
   operationalization of 31
Poverty
   measurement of 34
Prebisch, R. 120
Pryor, F. L. 13, 40(47:19)

R

Ranis, G. 4, 58
Rawls, J. 3, 11–13
Ray, J. L. 10, 18, 20, 75
Rockwell, R. 143
Rokkan, S. 3
Rosenau, J. 2

Rubinson, R. 3
Rummel, R. 4
Russett, B. M. 3, 10, 17, 23,
  23(46:8), 120, 127
Russo, A. J. 17(45:3)

S

Sawyer, J. 16
Sawyer, M. 3
Schiller, B. R. 17
Scolnik, H. 14
Scott, R. 35(47:17)
Scott, W. 25
Senghaas, D. 80(82:4)
Simon, H. 121–123
Singer, J. D. 10, 18, 20, 75
Skjelsbaek, N. 127
Smith, A. 13
Snyder, D. 166
Snyder, R. 166
Social Immmobility Index
  operationalization of 31
Sondquist, R. 57
Stallings, B. 4
Sunkel, O. 120

T

Taylor, C. L. 5, 21, 25, 25(46:10),
  38
Taylor, L. 60
Tilly, C. 166
Tinbergen, J. 9, 14
Tobin, J. 13
Tonelson, A. 15
Tucker, R. 128
Tufte, E. 63

U

United Nations 31

W

Wallerstein, I. 80(82:4)
Weiner, N. 102
Wilensky, H. 94
Wiles, P. 165(174:2)
Woodhouse, E. 1

Y

Yotopoulos, P. 89

WIDENER UNIVERSITY
WOLFGRAM
LIBRARY
CHESTER, PA.

DEC 2 0 1982

JUB 1 9 1983

DATE DUE

NOV 1 4 1990		
DEC 2 0 1992		
UG 1 0 1995		

Demco, Inc. 38-293